Cambridge Elements ≡

Elements in Politics and Society in Southeast Asia
edited by
Edward Aspinall
Australian National University
Meredith L. Weiss
University at Albany, SUNY

INDEPENDENT TIMOR-LESTE

Between Coercion and Consent

Douglas Kammen

National University of Singapore

CAMBRIDGE
UNIVERSITY PRESS

CAMBRIDGE
UNIVERSITY PRESS

University Printing House, Cambridge CB2 8BS, United Kingdom

One Liberty Plaza, 20th Floor, New York, NY 10006, USA

477 Williamstown Road, Port Melbourne, VIC 3207, Australia

314–321, 3rd Floor, Plot 3, Splendor Forum, Jasola District Centre,
New Delhi – 110025, India

79 Anson Road, #06–04/06, Singapore 079906

Cambridge University Press is part of the University of Cambridge.

It furthers the University's mission by disseminating knowledge in the pursuit of
education, learning, and research at the highest international levels of excellence.

www.cambridge.org
Information on this title: www.cambridge.org/9781108457583
DOI: 10.1017/9781108558488

First published 2019

A catalogue record for this publication is available from the British Library.

ISBN 978-1-108-45758-3 Paperback
ISSN 2515-2998 (online)
ISSN 2515-298X (print)

Independent Timor-Leste

Between Coercion and Consent

Elements in Politics and Society in Southeast Asia

DOI: 10.1017/9781108558488
First published online: March 2019

Douglas Kammen
National University of Singapore

Author for correspondence: Douglas Kammen seadak@nus.edu.sg

Abstract: This Element explores the primary modes by which rulers have exercised power and shaped political relations in Timor-Leste across four distinct periods. The contrast between coercion under colonial rule and consent expressed through the 1999 referendum on independence exerted a powerful influence on scholarship on Timor-Leste's politics and future. Since the restoration of independence in 2002, however, politics in Timor-Leste are best understood in terms of powerful economic constraints during the first Fretilin government (2002–2006), and thereafter, thanks to revenue from the country's petroleum reserves, a ruling strategy based on a wide range of inducements (rather than genuine consent).

Keywords: democracy, state-building, national identity, political economy, ruling strategy

ISBNs: 9781108457583 (PB), 9781108558488 (OC)
ISSNs: 2515-2998 (online), 2515-298X (print)

Contents

1 Introduction

Of all the rebellions against the newly independent states in Southeast Asia since the end of World War II, only one has resulted in the formation of a new nation-state: Timor-Leste. Demographic, military, and geopolitical factors were stacked overwhelmingly against the people of Portuguese Timor, as were the deprivations under a brutal 24-year occupation; but one factor loomed inordinately in their favor – the legal niceties of international law on colonial rule and self-determination. For despite the Indonesian invasion in late 1975 and de facto recognition of its annexation accorded by many governments, Portuguese Timor remained on the United Nations list of non-decolonized territories, with Portugal still recognized as the legal authority.[1]

The success of the East Timorese people's painful struggle for independence was a function of a fortuitous conjuncture at the end of the Cold War. On the one hand, the fall of the Berlin Wall in 1989 set off a chain reaction of democratic uprisings that resulted in the birth of six new states out of the former Yugoslavia and fifteen new states out of the former Soviet Union. Beyond Europe, the decade also saw the formation of newly independent states in Namibia, Eritrea, Palau, and Micronesia. This flurry of new sovereign states set a critical precedent that encouraged powerholders in Washington and elsewhere to imagine extending the principle of self-determination to the people of Timor-Leste. On the other hand, the Clinton-era turn to internationalism made possible an unprecedented expansion in UN engagement and missions around the world. But this was accompanied by military disaster in Somalia in 1992, failure to act to prevent genocide in Rwanda in 1994, and cover for US unilateralism in the Balkans thereafter. For this reason, the UN was desperate for a success story, and no territory provided more favorable conditions for the UN to play midwife to the creation of a new nation-state than occupied East Timor.

Release from Indonesian rule came at a high cost. In response to an agreement brokered by the UN for a referendum on the future of the territory, the Indonesian military and its civilian militias waged a horrific campaign of intimidation and violence. Despite this, on August 30, 1999, the people of Timor-Leste voted overwhelmingly for independence. A final spasm of violence caused mass devastation to the territory's infrastructure and the movement – both voluntary and forced – of hundreds of thousands of people across

---

[1] This volume will use Portuguese Timor when discussing the territory under Portuguese colonial rule (to 1975), East Timor when referring to the territory while under Indonesian occupation (1976–1999), and Timor-Leste for the period under UN-tutelage and since the achievement of independence in 2002. The people of the territory are referred to as East Timorese (so as to avoid any confusion with the people in the Indonesian province of West Timor).

the border to Indonesian West Timor. With the flight of Indonesian officials, there was a total collapse of state institutions.

The referendum and violence in 1999 gave rise to two closely related perspectives on Timor-Leste. The first, highlighting the nation, was a linear narrative from colonial exploitation and neocolonial violence to national unity and the corresponding goodwill of the "international community." It is the story of the power of ideals and the victory of consent. The second perspective, privileging statehood, portrayed Timor-Leste as a blank slate on which the UN would undertake the construction of entirely new state institutions and establish the conditions for a democratic future. These two perspectives have exerted considerable influence over interpretations of politics in Timor-Leste since independence. But both were simplistic, and at times self-serving. The black-and-white depiction of a movement from domination to consent erases the specificity of conditions: elite collaboration with Portuguese colonial rule and the late emergence of nationalism; the bitter internal political conflicts and transformations of the armed struggle against the Indonesian occupation; generational change and newly emergent political cleavages. And while the Indonesian state in the occupied territory did collapse, it did not follow that Timor-Leste was a blank slate. During the long Indonesian occupation, East Timorese had developed significant institutions and ideas about their own future. They wanted protection and assistance on the road to independence, but did not want to be invigilated by the United Nations.

What sort of politics would emerge in newly independent Timor-Leste? Where some observers were optimistic the country would readily adopt and adapt to democratic norms and find a niche in global markets, others feared the simultaneous challenges of state-building, democratization, and economic reconstruction would prove too much. More specifically, we might begin by asking:

- What sort of regime has emerged since the restoration of independence in 2002?
- What dynamics have shaped Timor-Leste's economy and what are its prospects?
- What are the bases of identity, mobilization, and political engagement?

Answers to these questions have varied greatly, but four major approaches can be identified. The first, and by far the most common, approach stems from the indisputable fact that the 1999 referendum marked a fundamental point of rupture and the subsequent UN mission the guarantee of independence. This spawned a large body of scholarship on state-building in which the UN and/or East Timorese actors are depicted as either the source of state strength or weakness (Martin and Mayer-Reickh 2005, Goldstone 2004, Goldstone 2013) and a complementary but smaller literature on East Timorese nationalism, characterized by much the same binary in assessments (Babo-Soares 2003, Soares 2001). Alongside this, but with little cross-fertilization, a second body of literature emerged on questions of justice and reconciliation, based on the assumption that only by addressing the country's violent past would it be possible to develop a healthy civil society and a flourishing democracy. There are significant differences in concerns, of course, with some authors focusing on justice and truth-seeking (Kent 2012, Roosa 2007), others on the intersection and even hybridization of international and local models (Katzenstein 2003, Wallis 2012).

A third *problematique* posed in the literature on politics in Timor-Leste concerns the development and quality of democracy in general and elections in particular. Here, theoretical debates about institutional design (Shoesmith 2003, Feijó 2016) – the constitution, the semi-presidential system, regulatory frameworks, etc. – commingle with more empirical studies of political parties and elections (King 2003, Leach 2009, Leach 2013). The trajectory of assessments has oscillated across time and often along partisan lines between optimism, condemnation, and tempered praise. Against this, a smaller, fourth body of literature addresses Timor-Leste's political economy. Given that Timor-Leste has emerged as one of the most petroleum-dependent states in the world, it is little wonder that much of this analysis has been framed in terms of the resource curse (Drysdale 2007, Neves 2013). More recently, a distinct but complementary line of analysis has shifted the focus from the ways in which dependence on natural resource rents may distort state institutions and squander scarce resources to the clientelist logic of budget allocations and their abuses (Scambary 2015).

Timor-Leste has become neither the utopia some observers imaged nor the dystopia others predicted. Instead, it is a nation-state enchanted and bedeviled by politics – the promises of campaigns and the mundane aspects of administration, the opportunities and pitfalls of budgeting and contracts, and the search for identities old and new. In place of judgement and prognostication found in much writing on Timor-Leste's politics, what is required is an assessment of the balance of forces and dynamics that have made the country what it is today and a framework for further research.

To do so, this Element identifies the primary modes by which rulers have exercised power and shaped political relations in Timor-Leste across four distinct periods. While state *coercion* and popular *consent* neatly summarize the dominant relations of rule under the Indonesian occupation and the brief period of UN tutelage, respectively, they provide only partial and imperfect guides to Timor-Leste's politics since 2002. Between these poles lie two other modes of rule that involve neither the fear of violence nor the internalization of a dominant ideology. On one side, but lying closer to coercion, are *constraints* derived from traditional conceptions of allegiance or economic pressures that may result in a silenced or pliable majority. On the other side is the neutralization of real or potential opposition through inducements – which may be purely economic or involve political office – rather than genuine persuasion, which I will call *purchase*.[2] This differs from patronage, which links specific patrons to specific clients or constituencies, in that the benefits (or side payments) may target the population at large. Furthermore, patronage may proliferate in circumstances where coercion or consent remain the primary means through which elites exercise power. It becomes *purchase* when neither coercion nor consent is a sufficient basis for the exercise of power and the distribution of benefits emerges as the ruling strategy. These ideal types, it will be argued, provide useful lenses for understanding politics in independent Timor-Leste.

This volume argues that the resolution of the 2006 crisis provided the essential parameters within which a new ruling strategy emerged based on an uneasy combination of *purchase* (rather than readily given consent) and *constraint* (rather than the continuous application of coercion). In this, there is less separating the major political parties than their expressed animosities might suggest. Finite resources and the absence of acute pressures to use those resources wisely make for a highly uncertain future.

2 A Violent Past

There is consensus among scholars that Timor-Leste's past continues to exert a powerful influence on contemporary politics, but little agreement about the precise nature of those historical legacies. Responses vary depending on the issue at hand and the length of one's historical gaze. For those concerned with elite behavior and the potential for generational turnover, the aborted attempt at decolonization in 1975 looms ever present. For those concerned with popular understandings of the state and its proper role, the abuses of the Portuguese colonial regime pale in comparison with those of the Indonesian regime, but the burden of the Portuguese head tax may loom large. And for those concerned with the provision of basic needs

---

[2] This schema is derived from Antonio Gramsci. As will become clear, however, constraint may also operate in the other direction, with the exercise of power limited by institutional arrangements and economic realities. Also note that I have substituted "purchase" for what Gramsci termed "corruption" so as to maintain a clear distinction between the neutralization of opposition through inducements, on the one hand, and the conventional notion of corruption as dishonest or fraudulent conduct such as bribery and nepotism, on the other.

in nutrition, health care, and education, a grim past may provide the starkest possible backdrop to the promise and possibilities of the present. Above all, however, Timorese and foreign observers alike agree that the country's history has been characterized by violence – violence perpetrated during 450 years of colonial rule; the extreme brutality under Japanese rule (1942–1945); and the horrors of the 24-year Indonesian occupation (1975–1999).

2.1 Portuguese Rule

Portuguese officials and imperial historians have long celebrated the fact that representatives of the Portuguese crown established colonial claims on the island of Timor in the early sixteenth century and maintained sovereignty over the eastern half of the island for more than four centuries. Typical of founding myths, such accounts contain a kernel of truth around which much fantasy has been woven. The reality is that for the first two centuries the Portuguese crown did not have a permanent settlement on Timor and conducted its trade in sandalwood, beeswax, turtle shells, and slaves from Larantuca, on the island of Flores. When Antonio Coelho Guerreiro was appointed to serve as the first Governor and Captain-General of the islands of Timor and Solor and other regions of the South in 1701, he faced such serious resistance from the racially mixed and Catholicized community of Topasses that he soon abandoned his post. The next seven decades saw almost continuous unrest and rebellion, resulting in a fateful decision in 1769 to move the Portuguese capital from Lifau to present-day Dili.

The Napoleonic wars and Portugal's loss of Brazil in 1822 marked a low point in the Portuguese empire, and it was not until mid-century that Portugal made the first efforts to build functioning colonial regimes in its African colonies and distant Timor. By then, however, sandalwood stocks on Timor were greatly diminished and the territory served primarily as a penal colony and distant marker of former imperial grandeur. In an effort to revive its fortunes, the government in Lisbon appointed a succession of governors tasked with turning the territory into a profitable colony. To do so, these officials sought to wed the longstanding practice of vassal relations with indigenous rulers with coffee cultivation, modelled on Dutch practices in Java. However, the annual tribute owed by the kingdoms to the Portuguese regime, forced coffee cultivation, and trade restrictions prompted a new wave of resistance. The small colonial army and Timorese warriors drawn from loyal kingdoms were sufficient to quell outright rebellion, but full Portuguese control over the territory remained elusive.

The turning point in colonial affairs came during the long tenure of Governor Celestino da Silva (1894–1908), who launched a series of brutal pacification campaigns and gradually transformed Timorese rulers into functionaries in a new system of direct rule overseen by district military commanders. Silva's effort to transform colonial fortunes in Portuguese Timor culminated in the introduction of a head tax on all adult males in 1908 that, it was hoped, would force subsistence agriculturalists to engage with the market and set the colony, which had long relied on subsidies from Portuguese Macau, on solid financial footing. Visions of efficient and profitable colonial rule were soon thrown into disarray by the republican revolution that overthrew the Portuguese monarchy in October 1910. Timorese rulers felt threatened by the abolition of monarchy and its symbols, and the announcement of a sharp increase in the head tax the following year prompted outrage from members of the lesser nobility now responsible for tax collection. Together, these forces prompted the last great uprising against Portuguese rule in 1911–1912. The rebellion was crushed at an enormous cost in life and property, thereby ushering the territory into an age of full colonial control.

Colonial rule in Portuguese Timor was colored in critical respects by the peculiarities of Portugal itself. Portugal's territorial claims, which stemmed from the age of exploration, had survived into the twentieth century in large part as a result of the protective cover of the "ancient alliance" with Britain. At home, however, Portugal's economy continued to be dominated by subsistence agriculture, with barely any industrial development. Officials in Lisbon promoted the development of profitable colonies but lacked the capital to make that dream a reality. In Timor, education was limited to the children of settlers and the indigenous elite. Health care was absent beyond Dili and two other towns. Roads were poor and shipping dependent on foreign lines. As a result, the combination of economic development, education, and print media that incubated nationalism elsewhere in Southeast Asia was all but absent in Portuguese Timor.

After two decades of shaky republican governments, in 1931 Prime Minister Antonio Salazar established an authoritarian – and increasingly fascist – regime that stifled ideas at home and investment in the empire. Undeterred, colonial neglect was celebrated in the semi-official ideology termed Lusotropicalism. With the onset of World War II, Salazar's declaration of neutrality was quickly ignored by the Allies and Japanese alike, with critical implications for distant Timor. Under brutal Japanese occupation for three and a half years, an estimated ten percent of the territory's population died unnatural deaths. Yet when the war came to an end, Portugal rushed to reclaim its colonial possessions. Whereas France and the Netherlands quickly found themselves facing armed movements for independence, there was no such challenge in Portuguese Timor. In the face of new international condemnation, the Salazar government promptly renamed these "overseas provinces" of a unitary Portugal. But cosmetic changes could not save the empire. India seized Portuguese Goa in 1961, and armed movements of national liberation soon followed in the Africa colonies. At the furthest reaches of the empire, under a mix of half-hearted developmental efforts and repressive security measures, Portuguese Timor survived as an anachronism in an age of rising Asian nationalism and Cold War pressures.

2.2 Decolonization Promised and Aborted

For the people of Portuguese Timor, change came in the form of imperial implosion in the metropole rather than a revolutionary upheaval of their own. In April 1974, frustrated by the unwinnable wars in the African colonies and decades of domestic stagnation, a left-leaning Armed Forces Movement over-threw the Portuguese dictatorship and called for immediate decolonization. In Guinea-Bissau, Angola, and Mozambique, revolutionary parties stood ready to claim the state, but quickly turned their guns on rival claimants, resulting in brutal civil wars. In Portuguese Timor, by contrast, there was neither a nationalist movement nor were there political parties. In this void, educated East Timorese rushed to form political associations ("parties" were still illegal) for the first time. The first to do so was a group of mainly mestizo civil servants who established the Timorese Democratic Union (*União Democrática Timorense*, UDT) on May 11. Nine days later a group of younger, more radically inclined Timorese formed the Social Democratic Association of Timor (*Associação Social Democratica Timor*, ASDT), which, modelling itself on the African nationalist movements and adopting a program of self-sufficiency (*ukun rasik an*)[3] and a common Maubere identity,[4] soon changed its name to the more militant Revolutionary Front of Independent East Timor (*Frente Revolucionária de Timor Leste Independente*, Fretilin). At the end of May, a third party – initially called the Association for the Integration of Timor into Indonesia, but subsequently changed to the Popular Democratic Association of Timorese (*Associação Popular Democrática Timorense*, Apodeti) – was estab-lished. There were ideological differences between the associations, but all agreed on the goal of independence from Portugal. In such a small setting, family ties between many of the founding members ensured a degree of civility and even the possibility of alliance.

---

[3] This was akin to Julius Nyerere's policy of socialist self-reliance and Kim Il Sung's *juche*.

[4] A common male name that Ramos-Horta used to refer to the poor, down-trodden Timorese peasant.

Less promising was the global context within which this hurried and poorly conceived process of decolonization unfolded. A decade earlier, the Johnson administration in Washington and its allies had applauded the military-led slaughter of leftists in Indonesia and rewarded Suharto's new regime in Jakarta for providing a bulwark against global communism. But in early 1973, with the signing of the Paris Peace Accords, the United States sought to salvage an "honourable" withdrawal from Vietnam. In this context, politicians in Washington and London could express approval for decolonization in the abstract but remain skeptical about the viability of tiny, under-developed and resource-poor Portuguese Timor as an independent nation-state. The possibility of an Australian trusteeship was mooted, but the Whitlam government was adamant that it "would not intervene again in land wars in South East Asia," adding that this applied "as much to the civil war in Portuguese Timor as to the earlier civil war in Vietnam" (quoted in Jolliffe 1978: 253). Outright incorporation into Indonesia emerged as a low-cost solution to the problem. To this end, Indonesian propaganda depicted Fretilin leaders as dangerous Marxists and suggested that an independent East Timor might become an outpost for communist expansion.

Indonesian intelligence operatives were also busy courting the newly formed Timorese parties, fanning their mutual suspicions while covertly providing light military training for several hundred pro-Indonesian Apodeti supporters. As a result, in early August 1975, UDT leaders staged a clumsy seizure of power in Dili and sought to detain their Fretilin counterparts. Most Fretilin leaders evaded capture and convened in the highlands of nearby Aileu, where they convinced the Timorese in the colonial army to back a counterattack. A month of fighting ensued in and around Dili. UDT leaders and their armed forces retreated west, eventually crossing the border into Indonesian West Timor, where they were welcomed as proof that the East Timorese people were incapable of governing themselves. UDT and Apodeti leaders also issued a series of proclamations opposing Fretilin and requesting that part or all of Portuguese Timor be incorporated into Indonesia (Kammen 2012). Meanwhile, with the outbreak of interparty fighting, the Portuguese governor and his staff fled Dili for the safety of Atauro island. Despite its insistence on an internationally recognized process of decolonization, by mid-September 1975, Fretilin found itself in the unwanted position of being the de facto government of the territory.

The Indonesian military responded to the political reversal in Timor by escalating its covert operations. Army special forces launched cross-border raids, and warships were deployed in coastal waters. By mid-October Fretilin's newly established Armed Forces for the National Liberation of East

Timor (*Forças Armadas de Libertação Nacional de Timor-Leste*, abbreviated Falintil) found itself engaged in frontline fighting. That a full-scale invasion was imminent was apparent to Fretilin leaders and western powers alike. On November 28, in a grim ceremony in Henry the Navigator Square, 37-year-old Fretilin President Francisco Xavier do Amaral, a former seminarian now dressed in military fatigues, read the one-sentence declaration of independence:

> Expressing the highest aspirations of the people of East Timor and to safe-guard the most legitimate interests of national sovereignty, the Central Committee of the Revolutionary Front of Independent East Timor – Fretilin – decrees by proclamation, unilaterally, the independence of East Timor, from 00.00 hours, declaring the state of the Democratic Republic of East Timor, anti-colonialist and anti-imperialist. (Jolliffe 1978: 212)

Diplomatic politesse typically precedes the violation of international law, and so the Indonesian response would have to wait another ten days. One day after the Fretilin declaration, UDT and Apodeti leaders issued a joint counter-declaration in English and Portuguese. The English version began: "In the name of the All Mighty [sic], and by the reasons previously referred, we do proclaim solemnly the Integnation [sic] of the whole territory of the ex-portuguese colony of Timor with the Indonesian Nation" (Soekanto 1976, 283–4). Of greater importance was that on December 6, 1975, US President Gerald Ford and Secretary of State Henry Kissinger were due to arrive in Jakarta on a one-day state visit. During their meeting with Suharto, Ford and Kissinger acknowledged Indonesian intentions regarding Portuguese Timor and requested that, for the sake of appearances, US-supplied military equipment not be used.

2.3 Occupation and Resistance

The Indonesian government rationalized its invasion of Portuguese Timor in December 1975 on grounds that it was restoring order, responding to the legitimate request of the Timorese people, and forestalling a potential communist foothold in Southeast Asia. Beyond these false pieties, Indonesian officials anachronistically claimed that the island of Timor had once been part of great precolonial Javanese empires, but had been separated by the chains of European colonial rule. In this view, the long history of rebellion in the eastern half of Timor was motivated by a desire to "return to the lap of mother Indonesia" (Soekanto 1976: preface). Thus, in his 1976 independence day address, President Suharto directly addressed the East Timorese people: "We view you as siblings now returning to the big family of the Indonesian nation." Certain of the righteousness of their own claims, Indonesian officials believed the invasion of Portuguese Timor would be easy, incorporation of the territory into the Republic of Indonesia uncontested, and the benefits of integration welcomed by the population.

But the Indonesian invasion on December 7, 1975 was poorly planned, clumsily executed, and faced far stiffer resistance than the generals in Jakarta had ever imagined possible. Fretilin leaders and much of the population retreated from the cities to the mountainous interior, where "base areas" were established. A civilian administration was called into existence to organize the population and, with a clear policy of civilian supremacy over Falintil, to direct the armed resistance. A war of position raged for three years. The toll on the population was enormous.[5] Under such strain, conflicts erupted between the civilian leadership and the military commanders as well as within the Fretilin elite. By late 1978, with the last major territorial base in the eastern sector under siege, Fretilin leaders allowed civilians to surrender. Tens of thousands of people were corralled into squalid "resettlement" camps, with little food or access to health care. With President Nicolau Lobato killed in combat, the Indonesian military declared that the resistance had been reduced to 100 men, whom they now called "a band of security disruptors."

Without international borders behind which refuge could be sought, and with no possibility of foreign assistance, the surviving leadership needed to assess the situation and reassess its strategy. A National Reorganization Conference was held in the mountains near Lacluta in 1981 at which Alexandre "Kay Rala Xanana" Gusmão was elected national political commissar and confirmed Falintil commander-in-chief, and the party name was changed formally to *Partido Marxista-Leninista Fretilin*. This had little to do with ideology and everything to do with ensuring a common set of analytical tools and the continued supremacy of the party. Only months later, the Indonesian military waged a massive "fence of legs" operation to sweep the island for resisters, disrupting food production and culminating in a massacre of fighters and civilians in the central highlands. Gusmão's (1982: 83) response was defiant: "We affirm that we are not many, but also that we are not just a few – *we are an entire people at war!*"

The resistance survived and new possibilities soon emerged. In 1982, Indonesia appointed the worldly Mário Viegas Carrascalão to serve as governor of the province. Soon after, in a daring operation, Xanana Gusmão managed to meet with East Timor's Apostolic Administrator Martinho da Costa Lopes right under the nose of his military escort. Even more remarkably, a series of low-level

---

[5] The (unnatural) death toll is estimated to have been between 102,000 and 183,000 (CAVR 2013).

meetings between Falintil commanders and Indonesian army officers that had begun in late 1982 culminated in a meeting between Gusmão and the Sub-regional Army Commander, Colonel Purwanto, at which they agreed to a temporary ceasefire (Kammen 2009). This was a political coup, providing breathing space for the resistance and an opportunity for Fretilin leaders overseas to issue a communiqué proudly declaring that they had won "the right to dialogue." The ceasefire soon broke down, however, and the Indonesian military set in motion yet another round of counterinsurgency operations and widespread rights abuses.

The conditions of Fretilin's survival and reorganization in the early 1980s encouraged two critical innovations. The first of these was the establishment of clandestine networks of civilians – some living under direct Indonesian control, others in more remote settlements – who provided the dispersed bands of Falintil fighters with shelter and supplies, collected intelligence, and acted as couriers. What had begun as a means of survival soon became the basis for wider popular participation. Gusmão's letters to the youth of East Timor bore fruit with the formation of new networks in which students played a major role in urban areas. The second innovation was a gradual reframing of the resistance itself. Between 1975 and 1978, Fretilin had claimed leadership over the national struggle and at times used violence against its rivals; a decade later, in a message written to East Timorese youth, Gusmão asserted that "participation in the struggle for national liberation is a moral duty, and above all it is a political and historical obligation" (Gusmão 1986: 86), and in 1987 he made the symbo-lically charged move of resigning from Fretilin and removing Falintil from the party structure, thereby making it a nonpartisan force open to all East Timorese. Reframing the resistance in national (as opposed to party) terms was strategi-cally brilliant. These moves also elevated Gusmão to a figure of mythic propor-tions who, it was said, could fly or turn into a white dog.

Over time, Indonesia rule in East Timor also adapted. The East Timorese were invited to vote in Indonesia's national election in 1982 and every five years thereafter. Following the 1987–1988 electoral cycle, President Suharto issued a new decree opening the province to Indonesians from elsewhere in the country and for the first time allowing foreign tourists to visit. Along with this opening, the Indonesian government encouraged foreign dignitaries to visit to see for themselves that the situation was peaceful and the province was the beneficiary of Indonesian developmental largess. These softer policies were necessary to assuage international criticism of the illegal annexation (Mubyarto et al., 1991), but also facilitated new forms of opposition. On the occasion of Pope John Paul II's visit in October 1989, young Timorese defiantly unfurled banners with crudely painted images of Xanana Gusmão and demands for an independent

Timor-Leste. The scene was repeated the following year when US Ambassador to Indonesia John Monjo visited Dili. A planned visit by a Portuguese parliamentary delegation in 1991 was cancelled, but weeks later clandestine organizers used a funeral procession for a young activist as an occasion to once again demonstrate for independence. When the procession reached the Santa Cruz cemetery, Indonesian troops opened fire, killing more than 270 people and injuring many more. Video footage of the Santa Cruz massacres, filmed and smuggled out of the territory at great risk, was shown on news around the world, prompting international outrage.

A year later, Xanana Gusmão was captured. Transported to Java, he was beaten, made to read a statement disavowing the independence movement, and eventually sentenced to a 20-year prison term for treason. Indonesia finally had their man. But as Gusmão had calculated, the media coverage of the massacre and his trial served to encourage young Timorese to continue the struggle and galvanized foreign criticism of the occupation and human rights abuses. From his prison cell in Jakarta, Gusmão continued to direct the resistance.

2.4 End Game

Gusmão had foreseen correctly that while it would be impossible to achieve a military victory (Gusmão 1986: 96, 1998: 228), the resistance merely needed to hold out until Suharto fell and Indonesia democratized, at which point East Timor would also achieve its liberation. The 1997 Asian economic crisis marked the onset of that end-game. The collapse of the Indonesian rupiah in late 1997 fueled hyperinflation, massive layoffs, and crippling capital flight. By early 1998, Suharto was forced to agree to an International Monetary Fund (IMF) bailout. Yet in March, the national supra-parliament obediently re-elected Suharto to a seventh term as president and Suharto appointed a new, crony-infested cabinet. Student protesters took to the streets. The initial student demands were for economic reforms, but eventually coalesced into calls for Suharto's resignation. Riots erupted in Jakarta and other cities in early May, and soon thereafter Suharto resigned, passing the presidency to his vice president and protégé, B. J. Habibie.

East Timorese seized on the political crisis in Jakarta. A month before Suharto's resignation, an East Timorese National Convention in the Diaspora was held in Portugal, at which representatives of Fretilin, UDT, and Apodeti agreed on the formation of a nonpartisan umbrella organization called the National Council for Timorese Resistance (*Conselho Nacional de Resistência Timorense*, CNRT) and the adoption of a Magna Carta concerning Freedoms, Rights, Duties and Guarantees for the People of East Timor (CNRT 1998).

Meanwhile, activists and students within the territory bravely staged free speech fora and demonstrations. President Habibie responded to pro-independence demands by suggesting that the province be granted "special status" and "wide-ranging autonomy." In August the Indonesian and Portuguese foreign ministers agreed to discuss the offer, but they continued to hold diametrically opposed views on the meaning of autonomy: "While for Indonesia this autonomy would be the final dispensation, Portugal was willing to consider autonomy only as an interim or transitional arrangement pending the eventual exercise by the people of East Timor of their right to self-determination" (ibid.).

Uncertainty in Jakarta and the outpouring of pro-independence activity made the province virtually ungovernable. Pro-integration figures and the Indonesian military responded by organizing paramilitary groups. The situation on the ground made it increasingly apparent how little support there was among the East Timorese for autonomy, a point the Personal Representative of the UN secretary General for East Timor, Jamsheed Marker, and Australian Prime Minister John Howard impressed on President Habibie. In January 1999, President Habibie made a surprise announcement that he would make a final offer of "broad autonomy" for East Timor. A "yes" vote would mean the territory would remain part of Indonesia; rejection implied that independence would be granted. Despite opposition from the military, by April 1999 Indonesia had worked out the framework for the Special Autonomous Region of East Timor that included the creation of an East Timorese Regional Council, police, and judiciary, but with Indonesia maintaining responsibility for external defense and monetary and fiscal policy. Negotiations in New York led to an agreement that the offer of SARET be made via a direct popular ballot to be administered by a United Nations Mission in East Timor (UNAMET), but with Indonesia responsible for security (UN 1999).

Well before the New York agreement, the Indonesian military and its district-level paramilitary groups began a campaign to intimidate the popu-lation. The use of violence intensified in the weeks following the New York agreement, including the massacre of at least fifty people at a church in Liquica district. Militia leaders openly called for "a cleansing of the traitors of integration." The Indonesian military, Geoffrey Robinson (2010) has demonstrated, was able to turn militia activity on and off at will, belying the generals' repeated claims that this was an expression of the genuine will of the Timorese people.

Despite two delays and massive violence, on August 30 the people of East Timor flooded to the polling stations and voted overwhelmingly (78.5 percent) in favor of independence. The military had neither done enough to win the referendum nor enough to prevent it from being held. And so ill-conceived contingency plans were set in motion. Massive physical destruction was accompanied by murder, leaving a death toll of more than one thousand, and the relocation – often, though not always, forcible – of more than two hundred thousand East Timorese across the border into West Timor. The Indonesian campaign of terror, carried out in full view of world media, served as an exemplar of the territory's tragically violent past. The referendum and UN oversight promised a new beginning based on consent.

3 The Impossible Dream: East Timor under the UN

UN officials, foreign governments, and human rights organizations expressed outrage at the murderous rampage, forced removals of the population, and wholesale destruction of property perpetrated by the Indonesian military and its paramilitaries. The scale of the violence and utter disregard for the terms of the New York Agreement demanded immediate action. A week after the announcement of the referendum results, the UN Security Council approved the formation of an Australian-led International Force for East Timor (INTERFET), tasked with restoring security and protecting UN personnel and the Timorese population. With Indonesian approval secured, the first troops arrived eight days later, and on October 20 the Indonesian parliament voted to relinquish its claim to the territory. East Timor's independence was now assured, but the form it would take and the road that would lead there remained to be worked out.

While there was unanimity about the objective of independence, the interests and expectations of the UN and the East Timorese people were less perfectly aligned. For the UN, overseeing the liberation of the long-suffering East Timorese people would serve as testament to the global commitment to uphold human rights and the power of international cooperation. But there were also institutional interests at work. UN missions had proliferated exponentially – from three initiated in the 1970s and five in the 1980s to 39 in the post–Cold War 1990s. This expansion involved a movement beyond interstate peacekeeping to "second-generation" missions focused on mediating intrastate conflicts, overseeing elections, and providing humanitarian relief. With this came abject disasters in Somalia (starting in 1992), Bosnia (1993), and Rwanda (1994). East Timor provided the ideal situation for the UN to score a success: for with the Indonesian withdrawal from the territory, there was neither an existing state nor competing armed factions. East Timor, in the eyes of the UN, was a blank slate.

In East Timorese eyes, however, this was a gross misrepresentation. Gusmão's efforts in the 1980s had opened the door for a more inclusive struggle for national liberation and even collaboration between elites long divided over the conflict in 1975. The final fruit of this policy came in 1998 with the establishment of the National Council of Timorese Resistance (CNRT) and the adoption of a Magna Carta of rights and first principles intended to provide the basis for the establishment of a sovereign state. The notion that East Timor was a blank slate was also at odds with popular Timorese ideas about what the end of the occupation would bring. There were widely held beliefs among East Timorese that with freedom would come prosperity: those who had made sacrifices during the occupation would be "paid" for their contributions (Traube 2007), everyone would live in a brick house, and a state of their own would provide for all. Against such utopian visions, Gusmão (1998: 231) had offered dire warnings not to repeat the history of other Third World countries where "the leader of the resistance will end up as president, even if he is not up to the task; guerrilla commanders will be generals and politicians will strive to become ministers. All because we were heroes; all because we suffered more than others! If this were to happen, it would be an outrage to the whole meaning of our struggle ... It would be a betrayal!"

3.1 UNTAET: The Denial and Emergence of Politics

In October 1999, the UN Security Council passed Resolution 1272 (UNSC 1999) creating a new mission, called the United Nations Transitional Administration in East Timor (UNTAET). Given the circumstances, UNTAET's mandate was both broad and ambitious: (a) to provide security and maintain law and order; (b) to establish an effective administration; (c) to assist in the development of civil and social services; (d) to coordinate the delivery of humanitarian assistance and rehabilitation; (e) to support capacity building for self-governance; and (f) to assist in the establishment of conditions for sustainable development. The resolution authorized the mission "to take all necessary measures to fulfill its mandate" and concentrated these powers in the hands of the transitional administrator, who was empowered to amend or repeal existing laws and to enact new ones.[6] While noting the importance of consultation with the East Timorese people, the resolution was silent on the status of East Timorese representatives, including CNRT and Falintil.

There is a voluminous literature on the UN missions in Timor-Leste, beginning with UNAMET and UNTAET. Much of this is the work of self-serving UN functionaries and academics offering policy recommendations regarding the need for adequate funding, better assessment of local conditions, and intra-agency coordination (Suhrke 2001, Pushkina and Maier 2012). From the outset, however, there were institutional tensions. Unlike UNAMET, which had been

---

[6] Grefell (2009: 214) argues that the "poor model of the rule of law" set by the UN encouraged subsequent ambivalence on the part of East Timorese leaders.

run by the UN Department of Political Affairs, UNTAET was placed under the UN Department of Peacekeeping Operations and was headed by the Brazilian diplomat Sérgio Vieira de Mello, who had been in charge of the UN Mission in Kosovo. Wholesale adoption of the model employed in Kosovo resulted in a heavy emphasis on peacekeeping, leaving UNTAET unnecessarily hamstrung by the principle of impartiality and ambivalent about CNRT, "which, though not a sovereign government, enjoyed considerable de facto legitimacy" (Goldstone 2004: 85). There was also a tension within UNTAET between the demands of the short-term mandate to restore order, oversee reconstruction, and prepare the territory for independence, and the longer-term objectives of state-building, stable democratic self-governance, and sustainable economic development (Beauvais 2001, Gorjão 2002).

In New York, plans for the new mission were developed without meaningful input from East Timorese leaders, despite their best efforts to engage with the UN. In mid-October, Gusmão, in his capacity as CNRT chairman, had under-scored the aims outlined in the UN Secretary General's report and reiterated the need for "dialogue with representatives of the East Timorese people" and "for assigning East Timorese to positions within the transitional administration structures" (CNRT 1999: 3). To facilitate this, CNRT established its own transitional council and separate committees on planning, gender equality, and public service. Yet, as a former UNTAET official subsequently noted in a searing critique: "Although the organizational structure of UNTAET was shown to the CNRT, the staffing table was not, since embarrassingly it included no Timorese" (Chopra 2000: 32).

CNRT leaders had initially foreseen the transitional period under UN tutelage lasting for five years. The Security Council resolution mandating the establish-ment of UNTAET specified that the mission would be established "for an initial period until 31 January 2001" (UNSC 1999), but left open the final date on which Timor-Leste would be recognized as a sovereign state. In light of this, Timorese leaders adjusted their expectations to a shorter time frame, with consequences for how they engaged with one another. This was reinforced by calls emanating from some East Timorese that, based on the November 1975 declaration of independence, the UN should withdraw immediately and the original Democratic Republic of Timor-Leste receive immediate recognition. CNRT leaders thus faced uneasy relations with the UN alongside domestic contestation over legitimacy.

UNTAET's response to CNRT calls for greater Timorese participation in the transitional administration was tentative at best. Some scholars view this as reflect-ing a concern that Vieira de Mello and Gusmão shared about the need to maintain "national unity" and avoid an immediate, potentially precipitous, descent into competitive politics (Goldstone 2004: 89), while others attribute it to the institutional culture of the Department of Peacekeeping Operations and its insistence, borne of operations elsewhere, on maintaining impartiality (Suhrke 2001: 2). In December 1999, Vieira de Mello promulgated a regulation establishing a nonelected 15-member National Consultative Council comprised of five individuals from the UN, seven from CNRT, and three from other political groups. This body was tasked with providing advice to the Transitional Administrator, but its real purpose was to provide the appearance of representation (Gorjão 2002: 318). The National Consultative Council failed to satisfy calls for Timorization, nor did an April 2000 proposal to appoint Timorese to serve as deputy district administrators assuage Timorese frustrations.

By May 2000, when CNRT convened a conference to discuss the path toward independence, long-time East Timorese spokesman José Ramos-Horta publicly "demanded the removal of all district administrators by August and their replacement with local leaders, as well as a fixed date for the UN's departure" (Chopra 2000: 33). But it was not until July that UNTAET replaced the National Consultative Council with a new 33-member National Council together with an eight-member Cabinet of the Transitional Government, half of whom were Timorese. Yet, as Feijó (2016: 143) rightly notes, "the sentiment that 'ownership of the process' was in foreign hands did not subside." Jarat Chopra, who resigned in protest from his position as head of the UNTAET Office of District Administration, charged that the UN "kingdom in East Timor" lacked democratic separation of powers and accountability to the people it was intended to serve (Chopra 2000). Other scholars have termed the UN approach to Timor-Leste "benevolent despotism" (Beauvais 2001), "benevolent autocracy" (Chesterman 2004), and "benign colonialism" (Kingsbury 2009).

The creation of the National Consultative Council was a much-needed gesture toward greater Timorese participation in, if not outright ownership of, the political process. But it came with political costs. Shortly thereafter, balking at Gusmão's leadership, frustrated by the limitations of its influence, and with an eye to the coming of competitive elections, Fretilin withdrew from the council.

The Constituent Assembly and the Constitution

No issue was fraught with more uncertainty than that of adopting a constitution. Two potential constitutional models emerged during the second half of 2000. The first, clearly favored by East Timorese members of the new National Council, was for a longer time frame with a constitutional convention that would ensure the widest possible participation in the drafting process. A longer time frame was particularly favored by Gusmão, Ramos-Horta, and others concerned about Fretilin's organizational advantages on the ground. The second model, favored by some high-ranking UN officials in light of the short mission mandate, was for an appointed constitutional commission (Devereaux 2015; Feijó 2016: 141–149). In the end, all actors agreed that legitimacy of the process would best be served by competitive elections for a constitutional assembly. The outcome was a compromise: for the UN, a new constitution would vindicate its trusteeship, while the short time frame promised a prompt exit; for East Timorese, the achievement of the "impossible dream" of independence outweighed most concerns about the time frame or the potential for the emergence of factional politics.

In March 2000, UNTAET promulgated a regulation for the election of a 75-seat constitutional assembly (later expanded to 88 seats) to be held on August 30, symbolically selected because it was the second anniversary of the referendum. A mixed electoral system was adopted, with 75 seats elected by proportional representation and 13 district-seats, in which individuals not representing a party could compete on a first-past-the-post basis.[7] Once seated, the Constituent Assembly would be allowed a mere 90 days to produce a constitution. This regulation, Anthony Goldstone (2004: 88) argues, supercharged Timorese politics, for in a five-month period "civil, party, and voter registrations were to take place, followed by a civic education program and constitutional commission hearings, an election campaign, and then the election itself."

Sixteen political parties registered to compete in the election for the Constituent Assembly, held on August 30, 2001. Of these, four traced their roots directly to the 1974–1975 period: Fretilin, which had been in continuous existence; the Timorese Social Democratic Union (ASDT), led by Francisco Xavier do Amaral, the first president of RDTL; the Timorese Democratic Union (UDT), headed by João Carrascalão; and the small monarchist Association of Timorese Warriors (KOTA). The remaining twelve parties had only come into existence in the weeks before the election, though most included individuals who had been prominent in 1975 or the resistance. The result was a victory for Fretilin, with 57 percent of the vote and 55 seats, followed by the youthful Democratic Party (9 percent, 7 seats), the Social Democratic Party (8 percent, 6 seats), and ASDT (7 percent, 6 seats), and other parties with only one or two seats each. The civility of the campaign and the high turnout (91 percent of the eligible electorate) were welcome indicators of East Timorese acceptance of democratic norms and the method for adopting a constitution.

---

[7] A proposal from women's organizations to set a 30 percent quota for female candidates was rejected because of opposition from within the UN and the new parties (Devereaux 2015: 22).

In fact, Fretilin dominated the constitution-writing process. A Fretilin draft, modelled in large part on the Mozambican constitution, had been in circulation since early 2001. Four other proposals emerged, of which only the Social Democratic Party's draft, in which a Portuguese constitutional scholar played a major role, was fully developed. Meanwhile, and against protests from civil society organizations and the Constituent Assembly, UNTAET insisted on the appointment of a Constitutional Commission tasked with holding public hearings (200 were held involving nearly 40,000 people) and forwarding recommendations to the Constituent Assembly. The final report of the Constitutional Commission highlights the protection of human rights and concrete concerns with land rights, natural resources, price controls for basic goods, religion, and social welfare (Devereaux 2015: 25).

The outcome of the Constituent Assembly, after a further extension of 90 days, was the adoption of a constitution quite close to the early Fretilin proposal. Tetum and Portuguese were recognized as official languages; November 28, 1975, was enshrined as the declaration of independence (meaning May 20, 2002 was officially the restoration); social justice was upheld; and decentralized public administration was specified. However, much was left vague, or at least in need of further legislation to be actualized. For many scholars, the most critical issue was the adoption of a semi-presidential system. This has been the subject of sharp criticism in English-language scholarship, with some authors expressing concern that a weak presidency would institutionalize political divisions (Shoesmith 2003). Portuguese authors, by contrast, charge that many of these scholars fail to understand semi-presidential systems, which have become a hallmark of the Lusophone world, and argue that semi-presidentialism may help "to bring pre-existing, deep political rivalries and in-fighting *inside the boundaries of constitutionally defined settings* – rather than ignoring their existence or attempting to repress their manifestations" (Feijó 2016: 226).

This debate was amplified in the months prior to the restoration of independence. In January 2002, the Constituent Assembly voted to transform itself into the first sitting parliament. Several of the smaller parties cried foul, believing that, if parliamentary elections had been held, they would have fared far better and thus reduced Fretilin's majority. The first parliament and government, they believed, had been stolen. Fretilin contended that the UNTAET regulation mandating the Constituent Assembly allowed for this outcome, and UNTAET acquiesced to the decision largely because it prioritized meeting its deadline for independence rather than on principled grounds of democratic accountability (*Talitakum* 34, 2002). Against this, the presidential election held in April 2002 pitted Gusmão, who received support from eleven political parties, against the ageing Francisco Xavier do Amaral, who publicly stated that he was running so as to give the electorate a choice. Gusmão swept the poll with 83 percent of the vote, with Amaral's support largely confined to Mambai speakers in the central highlands.

3.2 The Economy: Realities and Realignments

The violence perpetrated by the Indonesian military and its proxy militias in 1999 had devastated the economy. It is estimated that GDP fell by at least one third in 1999, and with regular supply chains disrupted, the prices of basic commodities soared. With the arrival of UN personnel and foreigners seeking business opportunities, multiple currencies – Indonesian, Australian, Singaporean, American – were in circulation. In response, UNTAET passed a regulation in 2000 adopting the US dollar as the official currency in the territory (a policy continued after the restoration of independence).

Donors committed massive amounts of money to support the mission and reconstruction of Timor-Leste. An estimated US$2.2 billion was spent during the UNTAET interregnum (October 1999 – May 2002), of which UNTAET operations accounted for US$1.43 billion, additional expenditures for peacekeeping totalled US$250 million, and assistance through the Trust Fund for East Timor and other sources US$512 million. "Unfortunately," La'o Hamutuk (2009) noted, "only a small fraction of this money came here to support the Timor-Leste economy. Nearly 90 percent of it was spent on international salaries, foreign soldiers, overseas procurement, imported supplies, consultants, overseas administration, etc." Even so, the influx of UN staff and peacekeepers, representatives of international development agencies, and nongovernmental organizations turned burnt-out Dili into a wild-West boom town. The streets were busy with new UN vehicles moving from UNTAET headquarters, where staff could purchase crates of beer, 5-gallon plastic containers of water, and imported meat, to the new supermarkets selling goods imported from Indonesia, Australia, and Singapore, and the bars and restaurants opened by enterprising carpetbaggers looking to profit from the UN bonanza. With housing in short supply, those who owned or simply claimed ownership over houses profited from easy rents.

Neoliberal assumptions about economics went hand-in-glove with UNTAET's promotion of democracy and human rights. In late 1999 the World Bank conducted an assessment of Timor-Leste's economy, concluding that "The great advantage possessed by East Timor is that it is starting life with a clean slate ... East Timor can learn from the successes and failures of other countries to put together a policy environment based on appropriate best practices from around the world" (quoted in Anderson 2003: 177). The World Bank was granted oversight of the trust accounts and other aid, and quickly developed programs to support poverty alleviation and the provision of basic services, the development of state institutions, and sustainable economic development with a focus on agriculture and the private sector (IEG 2001). To support these aims, UNTAET established a Banking and Payments Authority in 2001.

In Thailand, Indonesia, and elsewhere in the region, World Bank and IMF prescriptions for neoliberal reforms found a foothold with the 1997–1998 financial crisis, but soon ran aground on the shoals of powerful domestic interests and entrenched statism. In Timor-Leste, by contrast, there was no bourgeoisie or significant landed elite. Contractors could be valorized as the harbingers of individual initiative and micro-finance schemes, long the darling of international development, proliferated. Nevertheless, the World Bank (Rohland and Cliffe 2002) projected that Timor-Leste would be dependent on foreign aid to cover the government deficit for a few years to come. With most eyes focused on humanitarian aid, state-building, and the political process, aside from a few bland surveys of economic prospects (Hill and Saldanha 2001) and the occasional critique of neoliberal prescriptions (Anderson 2003), remarkably little scholarship was devoted to the economy during this period.

While policy makers eyed the prospects for sustainable development, two issues were of immediate concern. The first of these was land law and rights. UNTAET had decided to retain Indonesian law except where it contradicted international norms or was overridden by new UNTAET regulations. Land claims emerged based on four different bases: "traditional" claims, titles issued under Portuguese law, deeds issued under Indonesian law, and the occupation of land or dwellings since 1999 (Fitzpatrick 2000, Fitzpatrick et al. 2012). Efforts to address this situation were slow to materialize, however, and as a result of the enormous displacements at the time of the referendum and the many people seeking refuge or economic opportunities, the population of Dili swelled tremendously. The UN, its associated agencies, and international NGOs were hiring local staff, but generally required some spoken English or skills that were in scarce demand. To make matters worse, UNTAET and the World Bank had set targets for the establishment of a "lean" civil service. At the time of independence in 2002 it was estimated that only 22,000 people were employed in the formal sector (public administration, NGOs, and the private sector), out of an estimated workforce of 310,000.

3.3 The Security Sector

Arriving in late September, the force initially sought to disarm both the remaining pro-Jakarta groups and Falintil, despite the fact that Falintil was popularly regarded as an army of national liberation and had abided by the agreement to remain in its cantonment. When Falintil commanders refused to disarm, INTERFET backed down. Prior to the referendum, CNRT leaders had stated that an independent East Timor could adopt a paramilitary police force, on the Costa Rican model, rather than a standing army. Following this lead, UN Secretary General Kofi Annan issued a call for the creation of a Timorese police service but was silent on the status of Falintil or plans for a future military. Under UNTAET, new pressures came to bear on Falintil. On one side, donors supporting the reconstruction of East Timor insisted that their own regulations did not allow for the funding of "illegitimate" armed forces. From the other side, there was uncertainty about security sector design in the state-to-be. The resulting neglect precipitated a rapid decline in morale in the cantonments, and by early 2000 Xanana Gusmão declared that Falintil was "almost in a state of revolt" (Rees 2002).

While Falintil languished, UNTAET pushed ahead with plans to establish the East Timor National Police (PNTL). The recruitment process, which was overseen by UN police lacking local knowledge and sensitivities, came under fire for accepting several hundred individuals who had served in the Indonesian police force and for the dominance of individuals from the western districts appointed to the senior ranks. Meanwhile, UNTAET commissioned the Centre for Defence Studies at King's College, London, to prepare a report on defense force options. The report identified three choices: (1) a force of 3,000–5,000 personnel, created around a core of 1,500 former Falintil guerrillas, with small naval and air force components; (2) a smaller army of 3,000, of which only 1,000 would be Falantil veterans, and no other service branches; and (3) an even lighter infantry made up of 1,500 regulars and supplemented by 1,500 reservists (CDS 2000: 47–56, Ball 2002). A modified version of option 3 won out, in large part for financial reasons, and UNTAET mandated the formation of the East Timor Defense Force (*Força de Defesa de Timor-Leste*, FDTL).

The creation of the new defense force was plagued by controversy from the outset. The selection of a name was particularly difficult. The initial choice of a name – abbreviated FDTL – reflected a desire on the part of both Gusmão and the UN to disassociate the new force from Falintil, which, despite Gusmão's reorganization in the late 1980s, many East Timorese still associated with Fretilin. In mid-2001, however, the Fretilin-controlled Constituent Assembly amended the name to *Falintil-Força de Defesa de Timor-Leste* (abbreviated F-FDTL) in the constitution (RDTL 2002, part 4, section 146). This was intended to appease those who viewed the abandonment of the name Falintil as a betrayal of the struggle for self-determination, but critics argued that the name change was intended to reassert the historic ties between Fretilin the party and the defense force (Kammen 2011a). Problems also arose over recruitment into the new army. Of the 1,736 Falintil veterans who applied to join F-FDTL, only 650 were selected to join the first battalion in early 2001. (A second battalion, made up entirely of non-Falintil recruits, was formed in July 2002, bringing the F-FDTL to full strength.) Critics charged that the selection process had favored officers who were personally loyal to Gusmão and involved a strong bias in the small officer corps for individuals from the eastern districts, to the exclusion of those from the western districts (Rees 2004).

Further controversy ensued regarding who qualified as Falintil veterans. In addition to those whose applications to join F-FDLT had been rejected, there were many more who had served in Falintil or the clandestine networks at some point between 1975 and 1998. Lip service was paid to the reintegration of veterans into their communities and the creation of employment opportunities, but little came of this. The issue of veterans was exacerbated by the maneuvers of Rogerio Lobato, who in 1975 had served as the first RDTL minister of defense but had departed prior to the Indonesian invasion, and whose brother, Nicolau, had served as president of the republic until his death on the last day of 1978. In late 2001 Lobato, excluded from the transitional government and without a base of his own, mobilized disgruntled Falintil veterans and unemployed youth into a paramilitary group called *Força Base de Apoio*, much to the dismay of the UN overseers and Dili residents.

3.4 Independence Restored

Despite lingering disputes over the meaning of independence (restoration or not) and sovereignty (full or still constrained by the continued UN presence and responsibility for security[8]), the buildup to May 20 was filled with anticipation and immense hope. On May 16, UNTAET head Sérgio Vieira de Mello held a ceremony in which he playfully presented a giant, tinfoil-coated cardboard key to a beaming president-elect Gusmão. Foreign dignitaries from around the world, including UN Secretary General Kofi Annan, former US President Bill Clinton, and even Indonesian President Megawati Sukarnoputri, descended on

---

[8] The UN Security Council established a new mission, UNMISET, to provide assistance in public administration, law enforcement, and external defense for an initial period of two years, which was extended for a third.

Dili. The independence ceremony was held in a dusty field on the outskirts of Dili. At the stroke of midnight, Kofi Annan declared "That a small nation is able to inspire the world and be the focus of our attention is the highest tribute that I can pay" (Hyland and Murdoch 2002). Paeans to the people of Timor-Leste flowed. In the words of Noam Chomsky (2006), a fierce critic of Annan and the international order, the struggle of the East Timorese people was "a remarkable testimony to what the human spirit can achieve in the face of overwhelming, indescribable odds, an achievement that should inspire hope as well as humility."[9]

The literature on the UN period has focused on the lack of Timorese participation in the transition to independence and the failures of state-building (Gunn 2007). If UNTAET was a success, Goldstone (2004: 95) concluded, "it was a success for the UN but not for the East Timorese." There is no doubt a large element of truth in this. But it applied primarily to elites and institutions. With a few exceptions, the populace continued to hold the UN and its peacekeepers in high regard, had little to fear from the pro-Jakarta militias or their backers, and remained optimistic about what independence would bring. Fear of violence was becoming increasingly distant. The contrast between the recurrent violence of Timor-Leste's past and the consensus among its people on a sovereign, democratic future could not have been greater. This contrast, amplified by the language of the United Nations and media reporting that celebrated Timor-Leste as an international darling, formed a unifying pair: oppression called for self-determination, violation for the protection of rights, exploitation for prosperity. The diagnosis was correct but the predictions sorely amiss.

4 Independence with Constraints

The defining feature of Timor-Leste at the moment independence was restored was neither force (which had characterized the country's past) nor consent (which was the hallmark of the 1999 referendum), but instead constraint. Speaking one hundred days after the restoration of independence, President Gusmão acknowledged the widespread feelings of frustration: "We constantly hear it said that independence has only been for some people and that independence has not yet reached the population as a whole" (Gusmão 2005: 16). Basic infrastructure remained to be rebuilt, government offices to be renovated, schools to be refurbished, rural markets to be reopened, livestock to be replenished. Timor-Leste was the poorest country in Asia, with 60 percent of the

---

[9] For a moving video about what independence meant to East Timorese, see "Ukun Rasik An – the meaning of independence," at www.youtube.com/watch?v=cSK9Hq5Zsd4.

population living on less than US$2 per day, 50 percent of the population below the age of 15, and life expectancy of 59 years. Media columns and even street graffiti echoed Gusmão's assessment: "after obtaining a homeland, it is time to liberate the people" (Sahe Institute for Liberation 2003).

The literature on politics in Timor-Leste after 2002 came to be dominated by a focus on state-building – the shortcomings of design, the challenges posed by limited human resources, and well-meaning prescriptions for future improvement (Goldstone 2004, Martin and Mayer-Reickh 2005, Borgerhoff 2006) – with a complementary, but always secondary, concern with national identity and *soi-disant* nation-builders (Sousa 2001, Babo-Soares 2003, Simonsen 2006, Kingsbury 2010). Informed, consciously or not, by the new institutionalism in political science, many of these analyses exhibit a strongly voluntarist streak: get the institutions right and desired outcomes could be achieved. But the challenges extended beyond institutions and the enormity of fulfilling basic needs. Economic constraints bore down on both the government and the population at large. A state with incomplete institutions and precious little discretionary revenue was perched above a population that, though burdened by deprivation, paradoxically suffered neither from the bonds of land-owning elites nor capitalist labor relations. The result was a largely silenced majority in the countryside, a shrill political class in the capital, and an easily mobilized urban poor. In this context, political parties provided a partial but increasingly coherent lens through which an assortment of old and new tensions came into imperfect focus and resulted in crisis.

4.1 Fretilin: Government without Regime

While paying lip service to the defiant language of self-sufficiency (*ukun rasik an*) inherited from 1975, the Fretilin government adopted a laudable 20-year National Development Plan with sensible short-term goals. This was drafted following popular consultations with 40,000 people across the territory, in which the top priorities identified were education (70 percent of respondents), health (49 percent), and agriculture (32 percent) (RDTL 2003a). From this, the Fretilin government specified the primary objectives to be the reduction of poverty and the promotion of sustainable and equitable economic growth, with a focus on education and health (RDTL 2003b: vii).

From the outset, however, the new government was faced with a legislative backlog. This was in part a function of the need to pass a raft of enabling legislation to bring constitutional provisions into meaningful operation, but also resulted from reluctance on the part of the Fretilin faction in parliament to bring contentious issues to the floor. It took more than a year from the restoration of independence for a Court of Appeal to be established; the Council of State and Supreme Council of Defense and Security, both mandated by the constitution, only came into existence in 2005; a law on village elections was not passed until 2004; and, despite an extensive study of options (RDTL 2003c), plans for decentralization were never realized. On many of these counts, Lydia Beuman (2016) argues, the powers of the presidency were forestalled or weakened. Conversely, when Fretilin did use its majority in parliament to pass legislation, President Gusmão was prepared to use his power to veto proposed laws or send them to the Court of Appeal for review. In 2002 Gusmão vetoed a Bill on the Modification of the Tax System, arguing that it would result in unnecessarily higher prices for imported goods; in 2003 he sent the Bill on Immigration and Asylum to the Court of Appeal, agreeing with civil society organizations that the bill would allow the government to deport foreigners or shut down organizations with which they worked; in 2005 he vetoed a Freedom of Assembly and Demonstration Bill; and in 2006 he vetoed a new penal code, which included criminalization of defamation (Smith 2004: 282; Beuman 2016: 62–65).

The greatest impediment to the Fretilin government's plans for reconstruction and development lay neither in checks and balances nor the growing rift with the president, but instead with the economy. The state collected little in taxes and when the new Timor Sea Treaty, negotiated under UNTAET, went into effect on May 20, 2002, the government had wisely agreed to save all revenue from the joint petroleum production area during the first three years, amounting to a modest US$42 million (La'o Hamutuk 2002). In lieu of its own sources of revenue, the state budget relied heavily on donor assistance. The resulting state budgets during the early years were minuscule: budgeted expenditures in 2002–2003 were US$55.6 million; in 2003–2004, US$62.2 million; in 2004–2005, US$63.3 million; and in 2005–2006, when petroleum revenue first became available, US$142.3 million.[10] Even with so little to spend, and almost all of that going for salaries/wages and goods/services, budget execution averaged only 90 percent of the total. In fact, additional development partner commitments dwarfed the state budgets (from a high of US$235 million in 2002 to a low of US$115 million in 2005), though most of this went to the salaries of foreigners in the peacekeeping forces, experts posted to assistant the government, and international agencies and humanitarian assistance (Neves 2011).

Constrained by small budgets and the government's own adherence to a lean and efficient government, some scholars have highlighted Timor-Leste's

---

[10] Figures on the state budget vary considerably by source and are complicated by differences between the proposed budget, the approved budget, mid-year rectifications, recurrent versus capital spending, and the end-of-year executed budget.

dependence on foreign aid (Hughes 2009) and the imposition of neoliberal discipline (Anderson 2003). Missing from these analyses, but well known to Prime Minister Alkatiri and his critics, was that the economic situation would change fundamentally once revenue from production sharing in the Timor Sea fully came online. With extensive foreign input and assistance, Timor-Leste passed a Petroleum Fund Act in April 2005. Key provisions were that all revenue from petroleum resources was to be deposited in the fund; transfers from the fund could only be made to a designated state budget account; the sum of all transfers could not exceed a ceiling set by parliament; and transfers from the fund were not to exceed the estimated sustainable income (calculated at 3 percent), "which is the amount that can be spent each year forever and therefore can be said to strike a good balance between the interests of current and future generations" (RDTL 2005).

While foreign scholarship on Timor-Leste's politics has emphasized the dilemmas of building a robust state, Timorese political actors and observers often cast the situation in quite different terms. Government officials frequently highlighted societal flaws. In 2003 Prime Minister Alkatiri charged that a "colonial" mentality persisted not only in the new police force, where concern simmered over the recruitment of individuals who had served in the Indonesian police force, but also in the general public (*STL*, June 3, 2003). Dismissive comments, often attributed to Foreign Minister José Ramos-Horta, that young Timorese who had graduated from Indonesian universities were nothing but "instant noodle graduates" (*STL* August 20, 2002 and September 12, 2002) – meaning cheap or lacking in substance – further inflamed passions and resentment against members of the Portuguese-speaking diaspora entrenched in the upper echelons of the Fretilin government. For domestic critics, the problem was not a weak state but that the government was already too strong and enjoyed a compliant parliament, something exemplified by claims that Prime Minister Alkatiri had said that he expected Fretilin "to rule for 50 years" (quoted in Engel 2015: 121).

4.2 Foreign Affairs

In contrast with the domestic realm, the new government of Timor-Leste enjoyed far more freedom of movement in international affairs. This was in part a function of the high regard with which national leaders were held: President Gusmão was feted as the leader of remarkable struggle against injustice,[11] Foreign Minister José Ramos-Horta as a Nobel

---

[11] Gusmão was awarded the Sakharov Prize for Freedom of Thought (1999), the New Zealand Order of Merit (2000), the Sydney Peace Prize (2000), the Gwangju Prize for Human Rights

laureate,[12] and Prime Minister Alkatiri was widely regarded as a capable administrator and respected negotiator. But it also reflected the distance – common in most countries, and in the case of Timor-Leste exacerbated as a result of the violently disruptive passage to independence – between the immediate daily concerns of most citizens and the state's foreign relations.

While state-building in Timor-Leste has been the subject of much critical writing, less noted is the success with which the UN ushered the new state into a world of norms. With membership in international organizations seen as the *sine qua non* of sovereignty, Timor-Leste eagerly joined everything from the Asian Development Bank to the World Health Organization and signed on to a raft of international treaties and instruments on rights, labor, migration and trafficking, female political representation, and international law. But there were also political choices to be weighed. On the first day of independence, the Timor-Leste Council of Ministers requested admission to the Community of Portuguese Language Countries, with approval granted in August 2002. Part of the common CNRT program in 1998, Prime Minister Alkatiri celebrated admission to CPLC as providing fraternity with and access to a historically significant network and assistance in the development of Portuguese, which had been declared a national language in the constitution. For critics, however, this was evidence of the dominance of leftist, Lusophone returnees in the government.

From the time of independence there were also debates over the merits of applying for membership in regional associations – looking west, the Association of Southeast Asian Nations (ASEAN); to the east, the Melanesian Spearhead Group. Despite lingering resentment about ASEAN's long-standing indifference to Timor-Leste's plight under the Indonesian occupation, economic considerations of trade with and investment from Southeast Asia held the greatest appeal. Even with the support of the Indonesian government, early lobbying was rebuffed, first from Myanmar over President Gusmão and Foreign Minister Ramos-Horta's vocal support for then-democracy icon Aung San Suu Kyi (Smith 2004: 288), and subsequently from Singapore, which seemed to worry that "under-developed" Timor-Leste would become an economic burden on the association.

Timor-Leste's bilateral relations were an area of diplomatic success but domestic controversy. Both President Gusmão and Prime Minister Alkatiri were eager to put the country's troubled past behind them and to establish

---

(2000), the Council of Europe's North-South Prize (2002), Honorary Knight Grand Cross of the United Kingdom (2003), and Portugal's Grand Collar of the Order of Prince Henry (2007).

[12] Ramos-Horta and Roman Catholic Bishop Carlos Ximenes Belo were awarded the Nobel Peace Prize in 1996.

warm relations with Indonesia. Disregarding calls from civil society organizations, the government was adamant that it did not wish to see an international tribunal for crimes committed in 1998–1999. In 2001 Timor-Leste and Indonesia reached an agreement on demarcation of the common land border, and after independence efforts were made to resolve lingering issues regarding one offshore island. In June 2003, Prime Minister Alkatiri visited Jakarta to pursue a free market border agreement and a visa-free policy for those crossing the land border (Smith 2004). At the same time, the Fretilin government established warm relations with the People's Republic of China, which promised to provide aid for the construction of government offices, and Cuba, which sent 300 doctors to Timor-Leste and provided 1,000 scholarships for Timorese to study medicine in Cuba (Anderson 2010). Critics seized on this as evidence of Alkatiri's alleged socialist or even communist leanings dating back to 1974–1975.

The most contentious foreign policy issue concerned maritime boundaries and petroleum resources in the Timor Sea. This was particularly difficult in light of Australia's de facto recognition of Indonesian annexation in 1976, which eventually facilitated the signing of the Timor Gap Treaty of 1989 that provided a border demarcation favorable to Australia. Under UNTAET, Timor-Leste and Australia had agreed on a provisional new Timor Sea Treaty that, coming into effect in 2003, assigned 90 percent of revenues from the joint-production area to Timor-Leste. But permanent delimitation of the maritime boundary, which had implications for control over petroleum reserves, remained to be worked out. Prime Minister Alkatiri, who led the negotiations beginning in 2003, pressed for an exclusive economic zone equidistant between Timor and Australia that would "give Timor-Leste a significantly wider area than the Timor Sea Treaty area" (quoted in Smith 2004: 189). After three years of tense negotiations, mutual accusations, and charged demonstrations, an agreement was reached in 2006 for equal sharing of revenue from the Sunrise oil and gas field (Schofield 2007).

4.3 Security and Justice Initiatives

Timor-Leste was independent, but it was not yet on its own; indeed, its sovereignty was not yet complete. With the restoration of independence, UNTAET was replaced by a new United Nations Mission of Support in East Timor (UNMISET) mandated to assist "core administrative structures" necessary to ensure stability, to provide interim law enforcement while the national police force was brought up to speed, and to maintain internal and external security, including border control. UNMISET's 1,250-strong police contingent retained ultimate responsibility for internal security until May 2004, and the last of the peacekeepers only exited at the end of the mission the following year. While there was concern that pro-Indonesia militia members in West Timor posed a security threat, there were only a few violent incidents in the westernmost districts. However, the continued UN presence resulted in resentment about foreign influence and became a rallying cry for radical nationalists, particularly those associated with the Popular Council for the Defense of the Democratic Republic of Timor-Leste (*Conselho Popular pela Defesa da República Democrática de Timor-Leste*, abbreviated CPD-RDTL), who had insisted all along on a return to the 1975 constitution. But the most important impact of the continued UN presence was that it simultaneously insulated the state from responsibility for certain functions while allowing problems to fester within the security apparatus.

In tandem with the establishment of UNTAET, the UN had promised to pursue justice for crimes committed in 1999. Civil society organizations and a UN Commission of Inquiry called for the establishment of an international criminal tribunal, but UN Secretary General Kofi Annan soon backed away from such a position on the grounds that the government of Indonesia should be given an opportunity to prosecute perpetrators within its jurisdiction, as it said it would. Unstated was a concern that an international tribunal would adversely affect Indonesia's own transition away from authoritarian rule and major states' relations with Indonesia. Instead, the UN created a Serious Crimes Investigations Unit in Dili mandated to investigate serious crimes – including genocide, crimes against humanity, war crimes, murder, and torture – and the Special Panels for Serious Crimes, comprising a mix of national and international judges, to prosecute cases brought before it. Over the course of five years, SCIU brought indictments against nearly 400 individuals before the Special Panels, with sentences issued against more than 80. Among the many shortcomings in this process, the most debilitating was that "the vast majority of those indicted, including several senior military officers, remained at large in Indonesia effectively beyond the court's jurisdiction" (Robinson 2011: 1019). Meanwhile, the pursuit of justice was further undermined by the trials in the Ad Hoc Human Rights Court, established by the Indonesian government in response to international pressure, which acquitted twelve of the eighteen individuals who were put on trial, with the remaining six acquitted upon appeal (Cohen 2003).

Alongside legal proceedings, in July 2001 the United Nations also established a national Commission on Reception, Truth and Reconciliation (*Comissão de Acolhimento, Verdade e Reconciliação, CAVR*). As its name implied, the commission had an ambitious agenda: outreach to victims of human rights abuses; community reconciliation in the districts; participatory community workshops to record the impact of the domestic conflict in 1974–1975 and the 24-year occupation; public hearings held in Dili that were broadcast on national television, including one that sought to promote better understanding between national elites involved in the party conflict in 1975; research into the history of human rights abuses in East Timor from 1974 until 1999, including a major three-part survey and quantitative exercise; extensive recommendations to promote reconciliation and justice; and the production of a final report. The commission's 3,000-page report was presented to President Gusmão in late 2005 [though it was only published, in Jakarta, in 2013 (CAVR 2013)]. Neither the president nor parliament took action on the recommendations, however, resulting in "widespread community disillusionment with the transitional justice process, and with the limited form of 'justice' it has provided" (Kent 2012: 16).

Transitional justice initiatives were accompanied by a parallel concern with the place and potential uses of custom/traditional law (*lisan/adat*) and its enforcement through ceremonial community gatherings (*tara bandu*) (Babo-Soares 2004, McWilliam 2007, Asia Foundation/Belun 2013). Just two weeks after the completion of the constitution, a national NGO held a workshop on the revitalization of *tara bandu* and the potential for it to be accommodated within the legal system (*Talitakum* 36, 2002: 11). A year later, at another conference, President Gusmão (2003: 4) praised the potential that *lisan* had for promoting reconciliation, but warned about the need "to clearly define the limits to which Traditional Justice must comply with and thus avoid trampling on the spirit of the law of a country or stepping on human rights." These workshops set the stage for a proliferation of studies of traditional conflict resolution, often informed by romanticized visions of Timor-Leste's history and social relations (Hohe and Nixon 2003, Babo Soares 2004), while also highlighting disjunctures between international, national, and local models and understandings (Hohe 2002, Kent 2012).

Proponents of transitional justice argue that only by addressing past injustices will it be possible to create the social trust and commitment to the rule of law on which democratic institutions ultimately rest. For Timor-Leste, the double tragedy is that justice for serious crimes was not delivered and reconciliation failed to set deep roots.

4.4 Economic Sobriety

International agencies had presented ambitious plans to stimulate economic growth and create employment, touting the centrality of free markets and the development of the private sector. The National Planning Commission (RDTL

2002: 58) also expressed tremendous optimism: "Provided the transition away from the United Nations period is successfully manoeuvered over coming years, the outlook for East Timor is very bright with the prospect of steadily improving and broadly based growth for decades to come." This sentiment was echoed by many young East Timorese, particularly university students and those working for international agencies, among whom there was widespread talk about the country's rich natural resources – including oil and gas, minerals and marble, timber, and coffee – and fantasies that this wealth would magically transform Timor-Leste into the next Singapore.

Even within the constraints of minimal annual state budgets, economic policy quickly became contested. At times President Gusmão joined the chorus pushing back against the neoliberal orthodoxy. He noted that "the concept of a 'free market' is somewhat inappropriate" and lamented the fact that "one US dollar enters the country and several leave" (Gusmão 2005: 54). Other times he stood in opposition to the government. When the Fretilin government proposed increasing the tax on imported goods from 10 to 12 percent, critics, including President Gusmão, misleadingly charged that a 20 percent increase in the tax rate would place an undue burden on purchasing power (*STL*, September 19, 2002). Collection of taxes was further undermined by the reluctance of border control officers to crack down on small-time traders and inability to act against sandalwood smugglers backed by veterans and, as some charged, even Minister of the Interior Rogerio Lobato.

But the real economic problems were more basic. In 2004, when the first census was taken, three-quarters of the active labor force was engaged in agriculture or fishing, and of that almost all was at the subsistence level. Only 3 percent of the labor force was employed in the private sector, mostly as shop assistants, hotel and restaurant staff, and security guards, while 10 percent was self-employed, either owning small businesses or even smaller kiosks. The core of wage employment was in the civil service (5.5 percent, including a large number of teachers), the UN (1 percent), and the NGO sector (2 percent), which together accounted for approximately three-quarters of all wage-employment (DNE 2006: 164). And these jobs were concentrated overwhelmingly in Dili.

Coffee – which is the country's most important cash crop, concentrated in the western highlands – was beset by neglect of small and large holdings as a result of the violence and disruptions of 1998–1999, high labor costs, and low international prices. Exports were worth a mere US$5 million in 2002, rising by US$1 million in each of the next three years. As a result, the country's annual balance of payments was grossly skewed. In 2002, non-oil exports were worth US$6 million against imports of US$226 million, and though imports declined by a quarter over the next four years, exports only crept up to US$10 million.

To make matters worse, non-oil GDP declined sharply in 2002 and 2003 (–6.7 and –6.2 percent) before creeping up in 2004 and 2005 (0.4 and 2.3 percent, respectively).

As Moxham (2008: 13) correctly explains, "the 'pull' of Dili's reconstruction boom and the 'push' of agrarian stagnation" led to the phenomenal growth of Dili's population. The result was intense competition in Dili over property and squatting rights and the rapid expansion of the informal sector. Yet, while East Timorese struggled to cope in the face of unemployment and impossibly high prices of imported basic commodities, international "experts" continued to applaud Timor as a success story. Despite the obvious economic hardship, on a visit to Dili in April 2006 World Bank President Paul Wolfowitz praised Timor-Leste for having "established its economy well" (UNOTIL Daily Media Review, April 8–10, 2006). The truth of the matter was that with the withdrawal of UN personnel over the previous year, the economy was suffering.

4.5 Identity and Mobilization

The outcome of the 1999 referendum provided the clearest possible expression of the nation that was nurtured through conflict, and that nation's desire for its own state. But identity is never reducible to a single dimension. In Timor-Leste, national identity was cross-cut at the micro-level by houses of common origin (*uma*) and marital relations between those houses; at an intermediate level by the administrative structures of rule (of which the sub-district was primary under Portuguese colonialism and the district under Indonesian rule); and interwoven with the networks of armed and clandestine resistance that were ostensibly national but irrevocably local (Soares 2004). The restoration of independence was accompanied by a revival of traditional practices, best exemplified by the reconstruction of sacred houses (McWilliam 2005) and in some instances a return to ancestral lands (Bovensiepen 2015). These practices were celebrated as revealing the resilience of tradition and the freedom to celebrate it, but they could also be competitive, revealing claims of local ownership, primacy, and even micro-monarchical supremacy. Between the local and national, and often linking the two, there was also a proliferation of identity-based networks with origins in the resistance (CPD-RDTL, Sagrada Familia, Colimau 2000, Força Base de Apoio, Falintil Combatante), the many politically affiliated university startups, and pure criminality (sandalwood smuggling, cattle rustling, etc.).

Meanwhile, the period of UN tutelage had created vast new political space and opportunities for nongovernmental organizations. With the arrival of foreign development partners, East Timorese established a wide range of new

NGOs focusing on human rights, women's rights and participation, the environment, and practical development issues, along with a national NGO Forum through which experiences could be shared, issues discussed, and solidarity encouraged. For all the good intentions, many of these efforts were marred by restrictive donor agendas and short time frames (Engel 2015, Chesterman 2004; cf. Wigglesworth 2017).

In the months after the restoration of independence, violent incidents erupted in a number of district towns – Baucau, Viqueque, Manufahi, Ermera, Covalima, Bobonaro, Liquica – involving veterans of the resistance (including both combatants and members of the clandestine organizations) and shared grievances about recruitment into the new security forces. These reached a crescendo pitch in December 2002 when a demonstration by high school students was infiltrated by unidentified parties and resulted in rioting directed against foreign-owned businesses and the home of Prime Minister Alkatiri. In response, President Gusmão called for Minister of Internal Affairs Rogerio Lobato to be sacked, and though three separate investigations of the incident were launched, no findings were ever released. The following month, an armed group attacked villagers in Atsabe, Ermera District, allegedly killing seven people. Dismayed by the failure of the UN peacekeepers to take action, President Gusmão ordered an F-FDTL operation that resulted in at least 90 arrests and reports that the military had committed human rights violations (Amnesty International 2003).

These security concerns exacerbated the emerging political polarization in Dili. Mario Carrascalão, who had served two terms as Governor during the Indonesian occupation (1982–1992) and in 2000 had founded the Social Democratic Party (PSD), charged that Fretilin was intent on setting up a one-party state (*STL*, October 21, 2002). A year later, frustrated by Fretilin's majority in parliament, the youthful leaders of the Democratic Party (PD) called for the formation of an alliance of opposition parties. Rumors soon circulated that PD and PSD were planning a coup. The emerging PD-PSD opposition alliance was to take on regional overtones. PD's basis of support lay in four western districts (Bobonaro, Covalima, Ermera, and Ainaro), while PSD was associated with Liquica (where the Carrascalão family owns a vast coffee plantation) and Dili. Fretilin, it was generally thought, enjoyed its strongest support in the eastern districts. These regional identifications were mirrored in the security forces, where there were running rivalries both between PNTL and F-FDTL and within F-FDTL. In early 2004 a new weekly magazine closely linked to the Democratic Party made the issue of discrimination with the military its lead story with the provocative headline "Westerners [Kaladi] vs. Easterners [Firaku] in F-FDTL" (*Vox Populi* 1,

January 29, 2004).[13] F-FDTL brass viewed this as an effort to undermine the corporate unity of the military. Prime Minister Alkatiri believed it to be a plot to woo the military into joining the emerging opposition bent on toppling the government.

Political polarization reached fever pitch in mid-2005 when the Catholic Church organized a 19-day demonstration in opposition to new legislation that made religious education in public schools optional and recognized abortion rights. Sensing an opportunity, PD, PSD, and ASDT announced the formation of a National Unity Front, leading to a heated exchange with Prime Minister Alkatiri (Kammen 2010: 262). When the 2005 village-level elections were held, Fretilin candidates won 57 percent of all village headships, followed by the Democratic Party with 10.7 percent, the Social Democratic Party with 6.6 percent, and "individual" candidates (some from ASDT, others genuinely nonpartisan) at 22 percent. Fretilin leaders declared that the result of the village elections proved that it still had majority support and promised to sweep the national elections in 2007. But the real impact of the 2005 village elections was to reinforce the perception of regional blocks, with Fretilin predominance in the easternmost districts and opposition strength in the western districts.

4.6 Krize

The fuse for this political tinder was provided by the ongoing issue of regional discrimination within the defense force. In January 2006, 159 soldiers presented a petition to the President alleging that officers from the eastern districts were discriminating against personnel from the western districts. As formal measures to address the problem faltered, more soldiers left their bases, eventually bringing the number of "petitioners" to nearly 600 – or 40 percent of the entire defense force. President Gusmão turned the matter over to Prime Minister Alkatiri, who then gave F-FDTL commander Brig. Gen. Taur Matan Ruak permission to dismiss the petitioners from the force. Returning from a trip abroad in March, Gusmão gave a fiery televised speech in which he stated that he disagreed with Taur Matan Ruak's decision to fire the petitioners, which, in his view, suggested that the military was the exclusive preserve of easterners while those from "Manatuto to Oecusse" (i.e., the western districts) were the "children of militia" (i.e., pro-Indonesian).

---

[13] Some observers mistakenly have taken *kaladi* and *firaku* to be ethnicities or as corresponding to particular linguistic groups (Mambae and Makassae), while still others denied the existence of the communal divisions altogether. For the history of these terms, see Kammen 2010.

The speech had an immediate impact in two ways. By so clearly and publicly undermining [Taur] Matan Ruak's decision … [it] open[ed] the way for further efforts by FRETILIN to make its influence felt within F-FDTL. And by legitimating western grievances, it seems to have led directly to attacks on easterners in Dili … By 27 March, seventeen homes had been burned to the ground and easterners were crowding onto buses to flee the city (ICG 2006: 8).[14]

In late April a five-day demonstration by the petitioners escalated into an anti-Fretilin rally and violence ensued. The leader of the Democratic Party, Fernando "Lasama" de Araújo, claimed that the military had massacred 50 civilians, which was patently not true, and that he had received death threats, though no evidence was ever produced.[15] In early May the commander of the military police defected to join the petitioners. Minister of the Interior Rogerio Lobato responded by distributing weapons to Fretilin supporters. During the period of May 23–25 firefights erupted between the former commander of the Military Police and F-FDTL, between civilians armed by the Minister of Interior and F-FDTL headquarters, and finally between F-FDTL and the national police. This violence, in turn, ignited the tinder that was the greatest legacy of the UN presence – the tens of thousands of people from east and west who, seeking something more than a subsistence diet of tubers, corn, and annual periods of hunger, had been drawn to Dili after 1999 seeking the material benefits (jobs and rice) of the long-awaited independence. At least 38 people were killed and an estimated 150,000 people were displaced (UNHCHR 2006). The deployment of an Australian force barely contained the ensuing communal violence in Dili framed in terms of *kaladi* and *firaku*.

The opposition coalition succeeded in forcing Prime Minister Alkatiri to resign (replaced by a Gusmão ally, former Foreign Minister José Ramos-Horta), but fearing all-out civil war stopped short of calls emanating from within the Democratic Party for the dismissal of the Fretilin-controlled parliament. The American ambassador, along with a number of his western collea-gues, applauded the putsch, seeing a victory over authoritarian Marxists. With the backing of a new UN mission, Gusmão and Ramos-Horta portrayed them-selves as good democrats who would wait for the scheduled 2007 national elections for a resolution to the crisis. This strategy, however, involved a conscious decision to sacrifice the human security of well over 100,000 people – *kaladi* and *firaku* alike – who were to remain in squalid refugee camps dependent on humanitarian food assistance. In this, they were matched

---

[14] The UN Independent Special Commission of Inquiry for Timor-Leste (2006: 63) chastised Gusmão for this speech, noting his lack of "restraint and respect for institutional channels."

[15] Foreign Minister Ramos-Horta accused Araújo of "instigating unrest." *ABC*, May 11, 2006.

by Fretilin leaders who were equally willing to keep *firaku* supporters in the camps as a bargaining chip in this new political game.

Civil society proved to be illusory. Nongovernmental organizations, which had been the recipients of enormous amounts of international funding and praise, quickly fractured along regional and political lines, long-time activists stopped speaking to one another, and accusations flew. International staff who had once touted the role their agencies and local partners played in Timor-Leste's success now blamed the East Timorese. There was a flurry of media reports, and then academic studies, charging that Timor-Leste was a "failed state" (Cotton 2007, Gorjão and Monteiro 2009). The most damning appraisal would come from the pen of Portuguese journalist Pedro Mendes (2008) in an article titled "Timor-Leste the Unsustainable Island," whose diagnosis began with the following five points:

1. Timor is not a failed state. It is worse. The national project designed a decade ago has failed.
2. The "Maubere identity" is a costly fiction.
3. The independent state is sabotaged by the resistance structures.
4. The ruling strategy for the society is included in the Penal Code. It is called extortion.
5. The Indonesian occupation was ruthless and Timorese leaders are dismantling with zeal what was left: dignity.

Frustrations rose in Dili. Gang activity proliferated and attacks on the temporary encampments for the displaced were a regular occurrence. The situation was exacerbated by limited food supplies. Timor only produced half of the rice it needed each year. The political crisis further disrupted domestic agriculture and marketing, and now threatened private-sector imports from Vietnam and Thailand as well. In 2006 the government allocated US$7.5 million for food purchases, with contracts for rice imports going to Fretilin supporters without proper contracting procedures (Kammen and Hayati 2007). By February 2007, as rice prices soared, residents in Baucau and Dili attacked government rice storage facilities, eventually directing their rage at UN and government vehicles as well.

Crisis – *krize*, as the situation came to be known – was an understatement, for there were now multiple, partially overlapping issues: the political standoff between Fretilin and the Gusmão-led opposition; the breakdown of the security forces and renegade Major Alfredo Reinado, who had slipped out of prison and taken to the mountains; one hundred thousand or more internally displaced people; and severe food insecurity. Resolution was bet on the national elections scheduled to be held in mid-2007.

4.7 Conclusion

At the moment independence was restored, Timor-Leste was characterized by an incomplete state and a government with contested legitimacy. Underlying this was a paradox of the present and the imminent future: the Fretilin government operated within severe economic constraints under which there was little job creation or capacity to deliver on practical needs, but with the knowledge that shortly before the next election revenue from Timor-Leste's offshore reserves would make possible far-reaching state development initiatives and, through the granting of government contracts, private accumulation. These were the broad parameters in which a host of tensions and contradictions found imperfect but intelligible expression along partisan lines of government and an opposition coalition.

The great tragedy is that violence broke out before elections could be held, that the limits of constitutionalism were tested before elections could provide a mechanism for resolution. Equally unfortunate was that the resulting conflict – personified in the President and Prime Minister – resurrected historical animosities from the aborted quest for independence in 1974–1975 and competing claims about historical legitimacy and allegiance. The resulting crisis, whose roots lay half-hidden in control over the use of future state budgets swollen with petrodollars, fundamentally transformed the government and political economy. Reflecting back on the first Fretilin government, former Prime Minister Alkatiri lamented "although we had elections for parliament and for president, and had a government, in reality we didn't have the state as an institution" (Engel 2015: 104).

5 Timor's Purchase

A year into the crisis, with tens of thousands of people living in squalid displacement camps and UN peacekeepers still required to maintain security, Timor-Leste prepared to go to the polls. From the outset, issues and programs were an afterthought: this was a referendum on the crisis and its primary protagonists. In the presidential election, Fretilin candidate Francisco "Lú Olo" Guterres and Gusmão ally José Ramos-Horta emerged from the first round in April, and Ramos-Horta swept the second round in May with nearly 70 percent of the vote. The parliamentary election pitted Fretilin against the loose opposition coalition that had emerged in 2005 between the Democratic Party (PD), the newly allied Social Democratic Party and Timorese Social Democratic Association (PSD/ASDT), and Gusmão's hastily assembled new electoral vehicle, the National Congress of Timorese Reconstruction (CNRT, whose initials cleverly echoed the nationalist umbrella organization formed in

1998). An International Crisis Group (2007: 4–5) report at the time commented that CNRT "has a poorly developed structure, no policies and little more going for it than its leader's charisma." Unstated but clear to all was the prize: the prospect of a vastly enlarged state budget made possible by the country's petroleum revenue.

In these circumstances, Fretilin's adherence to its practical but uninspiring 20-year program emphasizing health care, education, and agriculture paled against CNRT's audacious banners with the reappropriated slogan "liberate the homeland, liberate the people" and images of towering future apartment blocks along the coast and Gusmão in front of missiles, fighter jets, and satellites. Of the fourteen competing parties, Fretilin won a narrow victory with 29 percent of the vote and 21 parliamentary seats, followed by CNRT with 24 percent and 18 seats, ASDT-PSD with 16 percent and 11 seats, and PD with 11 percent and 8 seats. But Fretilin floundered in its search for political partners with which to form a government. President Ramos-Horta responded by calling on CNRT to form a coalition government (termed the Parliamentary Majority Alliance, abbreviated AMP) with Gusmão as Prime Minister (Leach 2009).[16] Fretilin leaders were outraged – Alkatiri declared, "[W]e regard the decision as a political and illegal decision. Therefore Fretilin will never want to cooperate with this de facto government in the future" (quoted in Guterres 2008: 366) – and violence ensued, particularly in the easternmost districts. An election most hoped would lead to healing had in fact hardened political divisions personalized in the contest between Gusmão and Alkatiri, institutionalized between the CNRT alliance and Fretilin, and expressed geographically between *loromonu* (the western districts) and *lorosae* (the three eastern districts).

The 2006 crisis had shattered the fiction of national unity, but Timor-Leste was neither a failed state nor had it become dependent on foreign aid. Since 2007, analysis of Timor-Leste's politics has been dominated by three lines of analysis. A first view, focusing on elites, is that political rivalries dating from the aborted process of decolonization and subsequent schisms within the resistance have hamstrung the country's political development and prevented the transfer of leadership to a younger generation (Nolan 2015). A second perspective, now dominant in the literature, is that with easy petroleum rents Timor-Leste has fallen victim to the resource curse (Neves 2013, Scheiner 2015). Against these, a third line of analysis highlights the country's improbable democratic successes (Feijó 2016), with Timor-Leste now heralded as the most democratic

---

[16] The official title was the Fourth Constitutional Government (2007–2012), and that which followed after the 2012 re-election, the Fifth Constitutional Government (2012–2015). For the sake of simplicity and to highlight the regime, I will refer to these collectively by the name of the Prime Minister.

country in Southeast Asia (EIU 2018). All three perspectives capture important parts of the story. Missing, however, is an appreciation of how peacebuilding after the crisis provided a template for the development of a new ruling strategy based on a wide range of financial inducements (some for the populace at large, others directed toward specific societal groups) and the appointment of influential actors to political office rather than on genuine belief in the merits of the government's economic policy.

5.1 Buying Peace

The AMP government's immediate program focused on the three outstanding symptoms of the crisis: the F-FDTL petitioners who had provided the spark for the outbreak of violence in April–May 2006; the large number of people still living in temporary displacement camps; and renegade Major Reinado, who was arrested in July 2006 but then broke out of jail with 50 fellow prisoners and took to the hills with an armed band of followers. The security situation was exacerbated by economic paralysis. While the issues varied, Prime Minister Gusmão's approach was relatively straightforward: "We had to make policies to buy peace" (quoted in Murdoch 2008).

Formulating a solution to the F-FDTL petitioners was complicated by the interests of F-FDTL commanders and consideration of east-west tensions. Prime Minister Gusmão and President Ramos-Horta proposed paying each petitioner compensation for unfair dismissal and allowing those who wanted to rejoin to be accepted back into the military, but this was rejected by senior F-FDTL officers on grounds that these men were "defectors." An agreement was finally reached to appease all parties: each petitioner was offered the equivalent to three years of back pay (about US$8,000) plus an additional US$1,500 (RDTL Decree 2008), while payments were also made to veterans from the eastern districts who had been mobilized by F-FDTL commanders as a counterforce during the crisis.

Meanwhile, Major Alfredo Reinado, who refused enticements to surrender and evaded military operations, remained at large in the central highlands. This undermined the government's claim that security had been restored and resulted in increasing friction among Prime Minister Gusmão, President Ramos-Horta, F-FDTL senior commanders, and the Fretilin opposition. It was not until early 2008, after an Australian operation to capture Reinado failed, that political elites reached an agreement to put Reinado on trial in absentia. This, in turn, prompted a standoff at Ramos-Horta's private residence on February 11, 2008, during which the president was critically injured and Reinado was killed. The government's official position, which was repeated in most international coverage, was that Reinado and his men had attempted to assassinate the president, while the same day ex-Lieutenant Gastão Salsinha, the leader of the petitioners, attempted to kill Prime Minister Gusmão. Australian intelligence and autopsy reports contradict this version of the events (Australian Federal Police 2008, Boughton 2008). In fact, informants suggest that Reinado had come to speak with the president about the government plan to try him in absentia, and then was ambushed. In response to the shooting, Fernando "Lasama" de Araújo, who became acting president, declared a state of siege and ordered a military operation against the remaining "rebels."

Equally difficult was the question of the tens of thousands of internally displaced people dependent on humanitarian relief coordinated by the Ministry of Social Solidarity and international agencies. A number of proposals were discussed, but in the end the government offered compensation ranging from US$500 for loss of possessions to a maximum of US$4,500 for the loss of a dwelling (Van der Auweraert 2012). These grants, totaling a reported US$255 million (*Timor Post*, May 7, 2010), eventually succeeded in emptying the IDP camps.

In fact, even before these deals were reached for the internally displaced population, the F-FDLT petitioners and Falintil veterans, the AMP strategy of rewards and purchase had already found expression. The very first measures taken by the new AMP-controlled parliament were to pass an enormous increase in parliamentarians' own salaries and approve Law No 1/2007 on the Monthly Life Pension and Other Privileges for Former Members of Parliament (Shoesmith 2011: 328). Rice also became a central component of government policy both because of the need to stabilize the economy and the political opportunities this presented. The AMP transitional budget for the period from July until December 2007 included US$6 million to ensure food security. This was to cover the distribution of free rice to displaced people; a new in-kind payment of 30 kilograms of rice for nearly 17,000 civil servants, a critical constituency recruited under the previous Fretilin government; and for subsidized rice sales to the general public. To meet the need for rice imports while abiding by a commitment to support the private sector, the government signed contracts with a number of well-connected businesspeople, including the wife of the Minister of Economics and Development. Further political mileage came from granting the rights to sell subsidized rice in the districts to select veterans of the resistance. In 2008, the initial budget for government contracts and purchases worth US$4.8 million was expanded to US$14.4 million dollars, triggering heated charges of nepotism and corruption and an even more vociferous defense from the prime minister (Kammen 2011b).

Nevertheless, the policy of buying peace succeeded, and in 2009, when village-level elections were to be held, the AMP government introduced the slogan "goodbye conflict, welcome development." Government spokesman Agio Pereira celebrated Prime Minister Gusmão's accomplishments and vision for the future: "Step by step, steadily, his dreams are becoming [sic] true, because they are not only Xanana's dreams: they are the dreams of a whole people" (Pereira 2009). In fact, a new ruling dye had been cast. Government largesse could be used to pay off potential spoilers, to provide side-payments (such as subsidized rice) to the population at large, to fund patronage to critical constituencies (especially civil servants and veterans), and to grant clientelistic contracts to cronies. The short-term policy of buying peace had become a general strategy of purchasing quiescence, if not consent. The strategy would proliferate as state budgets ballooned in size.

5.2 Priming the Budget Pump

The AMP government's economic strategy was the beneficiary of fortuitous timing. The 2007 global financial crisis, combined with China's insatiable appetite for raw materials, fueled a supercycle of commodity prices. Timor-Leste did not have the diversity of resource wealth that many people imagined,[17] but it did have significant revenue from the offshore Joint Petroleum Development Area. When AMP came to power in August 2007, oil prices hovered around US$70/barrel and natural gas was US$6/MMBtu; by the following May these prices had doubled. After a sharp drop in 2009, oil prices stabilized at US$80/barrel in 2010 and then rose to US$100/barrel from 2011 until mid-2014. The result was windfall income in the Petroleum Fund.

Seizing on this, the AMP government passed larger and larger annual state budgets. The first, full-year AMP budget in 2008 totalled US$348 million and was nearly doubled in a mid-year budget rectification. By 2012, which was an election year, the budget had increased almost fivefold to US$1.67 billion (see Table 1). While the size of the budgets ballooned, actual execution rates were somewhat lower, and the extremely high levels of spending in the final months of the financial year raised concern about accountability and the quality of spending. With 95 percent of the budget coming from the Petroleum Fund, withdrawals exceeded the 3 percent sustainable income rule. In 2010, when criticism of this policy from civil society organizations and opposition parliamentarians intensified, Prime Minister Gusmão objected to the "mistaken

---

[17] Many East Timorese believed that Timor-Leste would become a tourist destination that would rival Bali. Tourist arrivals have been extremely low, however, and most of those entering on tourist visas come to work for international agencies or in the private sector.

Table 1: Timor-Leste state budget: original, mid-year rectification, and executed spending (in US$ millions)

	Passed Budget	Rectified budget	Executed budget	Percent executed
2007*	116	-	97	83.5%
2008	348	788	483	61.4%
2009	681	-	604	88.6%
2010	660	838	759	90.5%
2011	1,306	-	1,092	83.6%
2012	1,674	1,806	1,218	72.7%
2013	1,647	-	1,080	65.5%
2014	1,500	-	1,400	93%
2015	1,570	-	1,340	?
2016	1,562	1,953	1,630	83%
2017	1,370	-	1,192	87%
2018	1,461	-	-	-

* For August–December 2007, before aligning the financial year with the calendar year.

Source: compiled from various Ministry of Finance documents and detailed explication on the La'o Hamutuk website. Note that there is some variation in the figures reported across official reports.

policy of savings" and even attempted to scuttle the need for parliamentary approval of the budget, but his proposal was blocked (Arnold 2010: 218).

The gargantuan increases in the state budget were premised on the notion that state investment would be "the motor of economic growth and development," with private sector participation included via competitive bidding on government contracts (Feijó 2013). Alongside this, the government sought to build a network of social security benefits to protect the most vulnerable members of the population and reduce poverty. Had the Fretilin government enjoyed such budgetary freedom to carry out state-led investment and social welfare schemes, its critics would have charged it with promoting a "socialist" agenda. Now in power, those same figures touted this as the roadmap to development. And they received foreign encouragement to do so. On a visit to Timor-Leste in 2010, economist Jeffrey Sachs applauded the government plan to use the Petroleum Fund to finance economic growth, even suggesting that some of the Petroleum Fund be moved from secure US treasury bonds, as stipulated by the regulatory framework, into equities. Timor-Leste, Sachs predicted, would "grow faster between 2010 and 2020 ... than China" (SMH, March 30, 2010). After two years of preparation, in 2011 the AMP government unveiled the final version of a 20-year National Development Plan (2011–2030) that Prime Minister

Gusmão boasted would bring Timor-Leste into the ranks of the middle-income countries.

As one of the poorest countries in Asia with an exceptionally high birth and population growth rates (6.6 births/woman and 3.15 percent population growth in 2007), Timor-Leste desperately needed investment in infrastructure, including roads and electricity, and programs to combat the high levels of poverty, maternal and infant mortality, and anemic agricultural output. It also required greater investment in education and health. However, the Gusmão government continued to "under-invest ... spending merely 14 per cent of its budget on these human resources" (Scheiner 2015: 83). To understand the policy choices that were adopted and the means to achieve them it is necessary to appreciate the particular political calculations. The social welfare programs served as side-payments to satisfy popular frustration over the limited fruits of independence. This began with a "cash for work" scheme introduced in 2007, and was ramped up with passage in 2008 of a pension scheme for the elderly (those above the age of 60) and the disabled (Decree Law 19/2008 on the Support Allowance for the Aged and Disabled) and a Mother's Purse (*Bolsa de Mãe*) program for female-headed households (Wallis 2015: 237). In its first year, the program for the elderly and disabled covered 72,000 beneficiaries; eight years later the figure had climbed to 95,000 beneficiaries, or 17 percent of the population aged 20 and above. The pensions and Mother's Purse were so popular that concern arose over fraudulent registration.

Other welfare schemes targeted specific societal groups. Primary among these was a pension plan for veterans of the resistance. First passed by the Fretilin government in 2006 (Law 3/2006 on Combatants of the National Liberation), this was revised by the AMP government in 2008 (Decree Law 15/2008), 2009 (Law 9/2009), and again in 2011 (Law 2/2011). This provided graded payouts and pensions, including scholarships for children, depending on the length of service in Falintil (ICG 2011, Kent and Wallis 2014, Wallis 2015). The number of veterans and their relatives receiving these payments rose from 2,000 in 2008 to 33,000 in 2015, with many more applications still in process and demands for the scheme to be extended to members of the clandestine networks (i.e., noncombatants). Yet another government scheme is for medical treatment that cannot be provided in the national hospital to be carried out through a transfer agreement at hospitals in Indonesia and Singapore, with a regular and VIP track. Due to complicated paperwork, often in the capital, this was more likely to benefit the educated and those with political connections.

The second arm of the AMP strategy, already alluded to above, involved the clientelist use of government contracts. These were not only granted to relatives of high-ranking government officials, but also to win over actors who may not have supported Gusmão, his alliance partners, or his new government. Rice contracts, for example, were spread to include individuals who had previously backed Fretilin. Veterans, including many from the easternmost districts who had Fretilin ties, received a reported US$78 million worth of contracts for construction of the rural electrical grid (La'o Hamutuk 2013), which most recipients promptly sold to Indonesian contractors for 20 percent of the contract value. Together, side-payments and contracts provided an ideal political solution to three distinct problems: they appeased a variety of actors, they required the least possible state capacity, and they pumped cash into the economy.

The Gusmão-led governments touted the country's economic achievements. Real GDP growth rates averaged about 10 percent under the AMP government from 2007 to 2012, but since then have hovered around 5 percent (IMF data portal). This growth, however, has been the product of state spending, with virtually no foreign investment and only marginal job creation beyond an expanding civil service. The very high early growth rates also came at the cost of high inflation and enormous balance of trade deficits (nearly US$1 billion in 2011). Nevertheless, with the 120-megawatt Hera power plant up and running and strong appeals to tradition, in 2012 the Gusmão-led coalition easily won re-election and former Falintil and F-FDTL commander José Maria Vasconcelos (nom de guerre Taur Matan Ruak), who received Gusmão's personal backing, defeated the Fretilin candidate, Lú Olo, to win the presidency. A bloated 53-member cabinet was installed, and annual state budgets averaged more than US$1.5 billion.[18]

5.3 Megaprojects

Capital-intensive development projects were the decorative centerpiece of development policy during Gusmão's seven-year run as Prime Minister (2007–2014). In 2008, after a questionable three-week tendering process, the Chinese Nuclear Industry 22nd Construction Company was awarded a contract to build a national power plant that would burn heavy oil, but this was soon cancelled after fierce criticism from civil society organizations and the World Bank. The project was then granted to an Indonesian company at twice the initial budget (Scambary 2015: 298). Another prestige project carried out by executive fiat around the same time involved the purchase of two naval patrol

---

[18] The new coalition government, which involved fewer parties than its predecessor, called itself the Government Coalition Bloc (*Bloku Governu Koligasaun*).

boats, which failed to meet the tender specifications, and a berth for them at the Hera port, which subsequently sank.

Larger still, and involving ongoing uncertainty, is a grand plan for the development of a so-called Petroleum Corridor along the less-developed south coast. Socialized in flashy public presentations and quickly prompting property speculation, this is slated to involve a supply depot and onshore refinery, a divided highway, and completely new towns. Total spending, however, has been curtailed, with only US$52 million currently budgeted (out of a total projection of US$291) for the Tasi Mane supply base near Suai.

The most fantastic of the megaprojects began with passage of Law 3/2014 designating Oecusse district, an enclave surrounded by Indonesian West Timor, a special administrative region and home of a Special Zones of the Social Market Economy of Timor-Leste (known by the acronym ZEESM). This project, which involves the construction of a major port facility, airport, and planned city, was handed to former Fretilin Prime Minister and long-time Gusmão adversary Mari Alkatiri (Meitzner Yoder 2015). Seducing Alkatiri with the prospect of unbridled budgetary control over his own dusty turf, Gusmão effectively bought off the leader of the political opposition. The long-term vision is for a joint public–private investment totaling US$4.1 billion, but the immediate focus was on infrastructure and celebration of the 500-year anniversary of the arrival of the first Portuguese explorers in 2015.

These megaprojects have been the focus of a recent wave of research by foreign scholars seeking to understand the political dynamics at work, the impact on rural societies, and the popular understandings and expectations about what such development should and will bring in the future (Bovensiepen 2018). What will come of these grand schemes remains to be seen, but it is likely that most will never be realized as first envisioned, if at all.

While capital-intensive development projects have received the most scholarly attention, it is veterans of the resistance who have emerged as the real megaproject. As James Scambary (2015) notes, "former guerrilla leaders continue to enjoy elevated social status and authority" and "constitute a powerful lobby group within East Timorese politics." The original 2008 budget included US$16 million for veterans, but with a mid-year revision that rose to US$40.5 million allocated for veterans (5.2 percent) (see Table 2). Budgeting ran well ahead of applications and vetting, however, and at year's end only US$4 million was actually disbursed, with the remainder rolled over to the following year's budget. In 2010, the initial state budget of US$660 million included US$24 million for veterans; mid-year revisions to the budget brought the share for veterans to 6 percent; and as a percentage of the end-of-year executed budget of US$758 million, veterans received US$49.9 million, or

Table 2: Timor-Leste budget allocation for the military and veterans (million US$)

	Total Budget	Original Passed Budget			
		Military		Veterans	
	US$	Total US$	percent	Total US$	percent
2007[*]	116	2.5	2.17%	2.0	1.72%
2008	348	13.9	4.0%	16.0	4.60%
2009	680	34.7	5.11%	15.8	2.32%
2010	660	17.7	2.68%	24.0	3.63%
2011	1,306	14.2	1.09%	82.7	6.34%
2012	1,674	22.0	1.31%	80.5	4.81%
2013	1,647	41.4	2.51%	95.8	5.82%
2014	1,500	34.8	2.32%	87.8	5.86%
2015	1,570	32.8	2.09%	137.2	8.74%
2016	1,562	28.0	1.79%	107.0	6.85%
2017	1,387	27.0	1.95%	105.0	7.57%
2018	1,461	20.6	1.41%	98.9	6.77%

[*] First AMP budget backdated to cover July–December 2007.

6.6 percent. The following year, the initial state budget allocated US$82.7 million for veterans (6.3 percent), but this figure fell in the rectified budget to US$72.7 million, and only US$45 million was actually disbursed, bringing veterans' payments to a more modest 4.1 percent of the executed budget. In 2013 and 2014 veterans were allocated 5.5 percent of the state budget, a figure more than twice that for the military, and in 2015 this rose to a whopping 8.7 percent, or three and a half times the budget for the military.[19]

It is important to put these figures in comparative perspective. Viewed in terms of international standards, the ratio between the military budget and the veteran's administration in advanced economies (e.g., the US, Australia) is typically 4 to 1 and undoubtedly higher in Southeast Asian countries, while in Timor-Leste the ratio is inverted. Viewed in solely domestic terms, the amount budgeted for veterans in the budgets passed at the start of financial years between 2010 and 2016 was greater than that for health and agriculture combined, and nearly equal to that budgeted for the Petroleum Corridor and ZEESM. Veterans had emerged as a megaproject in their own right because they represent a critical constituency, wholly out of proportion to their numbers

---

[19] The absence of foreign security threats obviated the need for significant expenditures on the military.

in society or economic contribution. In an important study of the veteran's valorization schemes, Kent and Kinsella (2015) observe: "What is clear is that the veterans' scheme is bolstering a vision of citizenship that is based upon a militarized identity. It perpetuates the idea that a person's role in the (armed) Resistance is a key factor in determining their status to speak as a 'legitimate' East Timorese and, consequently, their access to political and economic power."

5.4 Identity, Mobilization, and Coercion

Modalities of political rule or class domination may find expression in quintessential strategies such as a reliance on coercion or the internalization of a ruling ideology, but these never operate in isolation. In the case of the Gusmão-led governments, from the outset the strategy of purchase was interspersed with symbolic appeals to culture and tradition. In an effort to quell the 2006 violence, then President José Ramos-Horta initiated a dialogue between leaders of the myriad veterans associations, martial arts groups and gangs, resulting in peace rallies that drew on culturally resonant notions of reconciliation (Scambary 2009). At the same time, President Gusmão suggested that the ongoing violence was not a function of elite conflict but rather a symptom of the failure to carry out traditional ceremonies to decommission weapons that had first been used by East Timorese against fellow Timorese in 1975 and then against the occupying Indonesian military. Gusmão appointed regional committees to oversee ceremonial events returning sharp weapons to their scabbards and prescribed places in sacred houses. Echoing the cultural revivalism that had begun following the 1999 referendum, this appeal to customary practices provided a strategic prop to national identity that had been shaken by the crisis. Following the 2007 election, *cultura* quickly provided a new means for the prime minister and his cabinet members to relate directly to rural communities, and especially to elders, that bypassed the political parties and minimized the role of local civil servants.

The restoration of security and order by late 2007 owed as much to societal fatigue as it did to the return of international peacekeepers. Social movements were weak, if not wholly absent. The national NGO Forum, which had grown to more than 300 members prior to the crisis (Hunt 2004), lost cohesion and linkages between Dili-based outfits, and those in the districts withered. Many of the politically affiliated start-up universities were shuttered. Meanwhile, little progress was made on security sector reform (Wilson 2012). With the attempted "assassination" of President Ramos-Horta in February 2008 and declaration of a state of emergency, furthermore, the military enjoyed a revived role in national life. F-FDTL units were posted to the districts and soon became involved in internal policing. But relative quiescence did not mean the absence of interests or the bonds through which they might find expression. In fact, the post-crisis period was characterized by rising friction between the government and the many secret societies and martial arts groups spawned during (or in imitation of) the resistance.[20] In 2010 the chief of police claimed that CPD-RDTL and a group called Bua Malus were plotting a coup, prompting the government to threaten to issue a ban on these groups (ETLJB 2010). With the drawdown in the International Stabilization Force and UN police presence, violent incidents erupted in Zumalai in 2011–2012 and in Viqueque and Fatuberliu after the 2012 elections.

Exacerbated by the challenges to his vision of development and clearly not trusting formal institutions to resolve these cases, the Prime Minister resorted to executive fiat. In 2013 the government issued a ban on all martial arts groups, and early the following year parliament passed a resolution instructing the police to close the CPD-RDTL headquarters in Dili (*STL*, March 6, 2014). Also beginning in 2013 was an 18-month standoff with Mauk Moruk, a former Falintil commander who, having returned to Timor-Leste after decades living abroad, had formed a Maubere Revolutionary Council in opposition to the government. The prime minister eventually ordered a military operation in which Mauk Moruk and several of his followers were killed. The government and its supporters argued that firm action was required to maintain stability, which was a precondition for successful economic development. For others, however, what initially seemed to be isolated incidents became a pattern of increasingly repressive measures.

The use of the security forces was paralleled in the legal realm, where the government flaunted the separation of powers, ignored constitutional protections, and attacked the independence of the judiciary. In 2008, when the president of the Court of Appeal ruled that the extra-budgetary Referendum Packet worth US$240 million in local contracts contravened the constitution, he was dismissed from the service on a flimsy technicality. Freedom of association came under attack in the decrees on martial arts groups, as too did freedom of speech, when in 2014 the government tabled a draft law that would regulate media ownership, curtail journalists' freedom, and require foreign correspondents to obtain official certification. Ignoring the concerns raised by civil society organizations, in May 2014 parliament passed the draft law. However, President Taur Matan Ruak requested a review of the legislation by the Court of Appeal, which first returned the draft to parliament for revision in accordance with the constitution and then declared the final version

---

[20] On the origins and variety of "disaffected groups," including involvement in the 2006–2007 crisis, see Scambary 2007. On arms control efforts after the crisis, see Timor-Leste Armed Violence Assessment 1, 2008.

unconstitutional. The prime minister retaliated by calling for a judicial audit and the removal of foreign judges, employed to support the woefully under-staffed judiciary, who had participated in the review.

5.5 Corruption and Justice

The AMP government was based on an odd alliance of parties and included the appointment of "underworld figures" involved at one time or another in the resistance movement, martial arts groups, and criminality, many of whom had played a role in instigating the 2006–2007 crisis (Scambary 2015: 294). So, it was not surprising that the AMP government was soon plagued by charges of corruption and nepotism. The subjects of such allegations extended from Gil Alves, the leader of ASDT and AMP Minister for Tourism, Trade and Commerce, who had a hand in the early government rice contracts, to a number of recipients of poorly regulated government development funds, beginning with the extra-budgetary US$240 million 2009 "referendum packet" (named in commemoration of the 1999 vote on independence).

In 2009, Timor-Leste established an independent Anti-Corruption Commission, headed by the highly respected civil society activist Adérito Soares, with a mandate to investigate government corruption and conduct public education on the issue (Blunt 2009, Soares 2015). The commission worked cautiously during the first few years, but public information about who was under investigation and even indictments did emerge over time. At least eight members of Gusmão's cabinets were investigated. Minister of Education João Câncio Freitas and Minister of Justice Lúcia Lobato were convicted of corruption. Minister of Finance Emília Pires was due to go on trial in October 2014, but the trial was postponed indefinitely because of political interference. Opposition figures, journalists, and civil society organizations charged that Prime Minister Gusmão was actively protecting corrupt officials within his government. In response to such criticism, Gusmão submitted an official request to the national parliament in October 2014 requesting that members of government remain immune from prosecution until after the 2017 election (Leach 2014). Parliament rejected the proposal.

Presidents have also interfered with justice through pardons, one of the few real powers granted by the constitution. In 2008 President Ramos-Horta pardoned former Minister of the Interior Rogerio Lobato for his role in the distribution of weapons that contributed to the outbreak of the 2006 crisis. A year later, on the tenth anniversary of the referendum, the prime minister and president prioritized relations with Indonesia over justice and ordered the release of a militia leader convicted by the Special Panels for Serious Crimes. Ramos-Horta rejected the idea of an international tribunal for the crimes committed in 1999 and demanded that the UN Serious Crimes Unit be disbanded (Gunn 2010: 237). The pattern repeated under President Taur Matan Ruak (2012–2017), who, despite his expressed concern about budgeting and corruption, in 2014 pardoned former Minister of Justice Lúcia Lobato, who was serving a five-year term for corruption.

5.6 Pushing the (Political) Envelope

A number of authors have highlighted the stark difference between the Fretilin government, which, though not immune to factions and fractures, involved a degree of party accountability, and the AMP government and its successor, in which CNRT was a mere electoral vehicle for Gusmão, who operated independently of his own party and above his coalition partners. As early as 2011, Dennis Shoesmith noted that the prime minister displayed disdain for members of his own government, at times even "publicly humiliat[ing] coalition members of his Council of Ministers." The flip side of this, Michael Leach (2014) observed, was that "key decision-making involving expenditure often lay with the Prime Minister's office alone." The coalition that elected Gusmão in 2007 survived because opportunism trumped principle.

In the 2012 legislative election Gusmão's CNRT won 30 seats and, with the support of the Democratic Party (8 seats) and newcomer (and Fretilin breakaway) Frenti-Mudança (2 seats), enjoyed clear control over parliament. It was in this context of relative autonomy that Gusmão, who was elected to a second term as prime minister, made the surprising move of reaching across the once-bitter political divide to appoint several prominent Fretilin figures to positions in the new government, much to the displeasure of his own supporters. Even more remarkably, the following year Gusmão appointed former Prime Minister Alkatiri to head the new Oecusse Special Administrative Region and Special Economic Zone (ZEESM), with unprecedented executive power over a significant budget and the promise of much more in the future. Relations appeared to be genuinely warm, with photographs of Gusmão and Alkatiri embracing and even being carried across a river together on a palanquin, much like the regional tours by Portuguese governors of old to the kingdoms, by men in traditional dress chanting "unity."

It was in the midst of this political rapprochement that Prime Minister Gusmão stunned the nation by announcing in late 2013 his intention to resign from office, and a few months later set the resignation to take place in September 2014.

The reason given was to allow a younger generation to assume national leadership. Gusmão's plan, according to some reports, was to form a council of elders (*Conselho das Katuas*) – to which he would belong, and presumably head – from across the political spectrum that would provide direction to his hand-picked successor. But September 2014 passed with the prime minister firing fierce denials of accusations of corruption in his government and backing the repressive new media law. Then, to the surprise of most and worry of many, in early February 2015 Gusmão did in fact submit his letter of resignation to the president. A week later, in a carefully prepared and curious twist, the president installed Gusmão's chosen successor, Rui Maria Araújo, a medical doctor from the opposition party Fretilin and former minister of health, as Prime Minister of a new Government of National Unity. A new, slimmed-down cabinet was announced. However, as Minister of Planning and Strategic Development, Gusmão maintained control over critical aspects of the government, including "responsibility for planning, investment, infrastructure, procurement and other key sectors" (Scheiner 2015: 86).

Gusmão's resignation and the appointment of a new government to serve until the 2017 elections was the subject of a great deal of speculation. Some observers viewed this as a long-awaited "generational handover" and even a welcome move in the direction of national unity (Nygaard-Christensen 2016: 348–349). Other scholars argued that Gusmão's maneuvers were creating a form of "consociational democracy," or power-sharing, between former rivals, with the attendant risk that without an opposition there would be a loss of accountability (Shoesmith 2017, Kingsbury 2017). If entrenched, some worried, a national unity government would deny voters of a meaningful choice. But accountability had already been compromised, choices stifled. In fact, the heralded "national unity" should be understood not as a radical new course of national unity or an elite cartel, even if it had the external trappings of each, but as the logical extension of the existing strategy of purchase, first offered with ZEESM and subsequently to the opposition party in toto. Even with the emergence of President Taur Matan Ruak as the leading critic of government policy, who in 2016 compared Prime Minister Gusmão to Suharto (Taur 2016, Allard 2016), the result was the two least eventful years Timor-Leste had experienced in the last four decades, and. For many East Timorese this was a welcome respite, but it would prove to be an intermezzo rather than a new normal.

5.7 Conclusion

Paradoxically, while the 2006–2007 crisis exposed an underdeveloped state, its most important impact may have been that it crippled the celebrated claims, built of the resistance, about national identity and unity. From this emerged a regime based on material inducements – broadly distributed patronage and targeted clientelism, or what I have termed purchase – rather than a genuine commitment to the sustainability of the market-based model or a belief in the promises of future prosperity. This model was supplemented in equal measure with elections, which provide a veneer of popular consent [without, it must be emphasized, "tax-payer voters demanding financial accountability" (Scheiner 2015: 86)], and at times, too, the strategic deployment of the security forces and legal restrictions.

If this was the logic of the regime and its rule, it is also essential to underscore the specific conditions under which it emerged. Extremely low state capacity in the wake of the 2006–2007 crisis combined with a desperate need to provide humanitarian assistance and revive the economy. But what made the strategy of purchase possible was the massive influx of easy resource rents from oil and natural gas. This alone is by no means unusual. What sets Timor-Leste apart from other resource-rich countries, and more specifically those emerging from major periods of conflict, is the juxtaposition of a puny and anemic domestic economy and significant natural resource wealth *without* descent into author-itarian rule.[21] Under these circumstances, and particularly in response to the 2006 crisis, an array of subsidies, direct cash transfers, contracts granted to key domestic constituents, and capital-intensive projects became both economically feasible and political advantageous. A decade of quiescence ensued. Were Timor-Leste to have a century's worth of petroleum reserves, as Brunei does, the population might genuinely embrace this as a long-term development strategy. But Timor-Leste's reserves are finite and there is widespread concern among the populace that national wealth is being squandered without consideration for future generations.

6 Hitching-Post

Many East Timorese wondered if the "national unity" approach to governance would hold or if there would be a return to the contentious democracy of the recent past. There was to be plenty of political excitement over a short 12-month period, but in crucial respects this was to prove largely epiphenomenal, with little substantive debate about the uses of the Petroleum Fund, budget allocations, and policy priorities. Instead, it was about which figures would sit atop the existing ruling strategy and hold the purse strings. Nevertheless, significant new dynamics did emerge on the path to the 2017 elections, primary among which was a partial realignment of the party map and surprising rise of party coalitions.

---

[21] By contrast, in oil-rich Equatorial Guinea Teodoro Obiang has relied on repression to remain in power for three decades, and in Brunei Sultan Bolkiah has used pomp and personal benevolence to establish a degree of real popular consent.

The road to the 2017 elections was foreshadowed by the emergence of new political parties. In 2011, as the government tried to put a lid on the troublesome martial arts groups, leaders of one of the largest such groups (Kork) established a new party called Enrich the National Unity of the Sons of Timor (abbreviated Khunto). Although Khunto failed to reach the electoral threshold in 2012, its base in and appeal to disenfranchised youth bode well for the next national elections. At the other end of the spectrum, President Taur Matan Ruak had become increasingly critical of Gusmão and his government, foreshadowing his desire to move from the relatively weak presidency to the rough and tumble of parliamentary politics. With strong support from young intellectuals, many with foreign degrees, in late 2015 Ruak established the People's Liberation Party (PLP).

Eight individuals declared their candidacy for the presidential election to be held in March 2017. Of these, Fretilin's Francisco "Lú Olo" Guterres was an uninspiring figure who had previously lost the 2007 and 2012 elections, and during the first of these was the butt of scathing ridicule from Gusmão. And yet, in a sign that national unity might just prevail, Gusmão threw his and his party's support behind Lú Olo, who won the election with 57 percent of the vote to 32 percent for PD stalwart António Conceição. The real surprise was that two candidates could claim 90 percent of the vote, obviating the need for a second round run-off for the first time in the country's young history.

The campaign for parliamentary elections involved stinging PLP criticism of the incumbent government's performance and colorful displays of grass-roots enthusiasm, but by and large "the parties' programs were often short on policy details and [budgetary] funding commitments" (Aspinall et al. 2018: 165). The election was all about leaders, with the generation of 1975 still center stage. A vote for CNRT or its obvious allies was a vote for a continuation of the path forward Gusmão had laid out over the previous decade; a vote for Fretilin meant Alkatiri's return; and a vote for anyone else, including Taur Matan Ruak, was a shot in the dark for a new player and, just maybe, generational turnover. Of the 21 parties competing for the 65-seat parliament, only five met the electoral threshold (recently raised to 4 percent under a new law). The difference between the top two parties was a mere 1,000 votes, with Fretilin winning 29.7 percent of the vote and 23 seats, CNRT winning 29.5 percent and 22 seats, followed by PLP with 8 seats, PD with 7 seats, and Khunto with 5 seats. "Conditions," Rui Feijó (2018: 210) writes, "seemed ripe for the continuation of a 'government of national inclusion'." But President Lú Olo's efforts to encourage such an outcome fizzled, with PLP and Khunto demanding more than Fretilin would give and Taur Matan Ruak's pointed criticism of Gusmão ruling out a PLP-CNRT pairing. In the end, ironically, Fretilin was only able to lure the opportunistic leaders of the Democratic Party – which had once led the vitriolic attacks on Fretilin and for nearly a decade been loyal supporters of Gusmão – to join in a minority government with only 30 of the 65 seats in parliament. Trouble lay ahead. And with Gusmão leaving the country to deal with the ongoing Timor Sea negotiations with Australia, other actors would take the stage.

Differences had prevented CNRT, PLP, and Khunto from waging a collective challenge to Fretilin's right to form a government, but once the new government was seated, leaders of the three parties quickly rallied to establish a new Parliamentary Majority Opposition Alliance and, with great seriousness, twice voted down Fretilin's program. Even with veterans expressing support for the government (*Independente* October 25, 2018), by January 2018 President Lú Olo had no choice but to dissolve parliament and call for new elections to be held in May. For a second time in just over a decade, an Alkatiri-led government had been brought down. This prompted a rush to form electoral coalitions: CNRT, PLP, and Khunto formed the Alliance for Change and Progress (reviving the old AMP acronym); three political odd fellows created a Democratic Development Front; four small, left-leaning parties joined in a Social Democratic Movement; and even smaller players established a National Development Movement. Fretilin and PD remained unaligned, the former projecting confidence in its own abilities and the later opportunistically awaiting a chance to again join with the electoral winners. The campaign was characterized by great acrimony (one observer team referring to "injudicious and inappropriate language"), but outright violence was kept to a minimum. Voter turnout, which had dropped in 2012 and 2017, was a robust 81 percent, a five-point increase from a year before.

The result this time was a solid victory for AMP, which took 49.6 percent of the vote (34 seats), followed by Fretilin with 34.2 percent (23 seats), PD with 8 percent (5 seats), and the Democratic Development Front with 5.5 percent (3 seats). While Fretilin retained its strength in the easternmost districts and did well in parts of the west as well, its tally in Oecusse, where Alkatiri had been granted his fiefdom, plummeted. Suddenly superfluous, PD was also frozen out of government. In an unprecedented snap election, the East Timorese people had voted for stability. Taur Matan Ruak was elected Prime Minister, but it is Gusmão who is back in the saddle as the linchpin of a coalition of odd fellows. We can expect a general continuation of the political style, if not the precise program, pursued with such vigor over the past decade. But in crucial respects

Timor-Leste, like its famously sturdy ponies, is tethered to its utter dependence on petroleum revenue on a trail somewhere before a crossroads it knows it will reach – Gusmão's inevitable exit, as he is now 73 years old – but cannot yet see.

6.1 Horizons

Nineteen years after the historic referendum that freed Timor-Leste from external oppression and set it on the path to statehood, the political system and forms of participation that have emerged resist easy categorization. Timor-Leste is a small country with a very poor population and significant but finite petroleum resources. With smallness come politics that are both intimate and contentious. With poverty and the ravages of the past come demands for a better life and frustrations when progress is slow or uneven. The result has been neither the utopia some once imagined nor the failed state others feared – though, sadly, both images persist in media reports and commentary.

Timor-Leste has performed remarkably well in terms of adherence to the democratic processes envisioned by the population and stipulated by the framers of the constitution. It is the most democratic country in Southeast Asia in both the Economist Intelligence Unit and Freedom House rankings, at a time many regional neighbors have experienced democratic regression. Taking a longer-term view, it is useful to remember that after achieving independence most countries in Southeast Asia remained under a single head of state and/or governance by a single party for an average of about fifteen years before the onset of authoritarian rule.[22] Timor-Leste has surpassed its neighbors in terms of both power-sharing and democratic resilience. Equally telling is the comparison with other former Portuguese colonies, with which Timor-Leste shares important political legacies. Here, however, the sequencing differs, with radical nationalist movements in Guinea-Bissau, Angola, and Mozambique all waging armed struggles in order to achieve decolonization, after which there was one-party rule and, in two of the three, debilitating civil wars; whereas in Timor-Leste, a very brief civil conflict preceded an aborted process of decolonization and a new foreign occupation, which, because of its brutality and despite internal conflicts, resulted in far greater unity than in her African cousins and immeasurably stronger commitment to democratic governance.

---

[22] Burma (independence in 1948): two parliamentary elections, three AFPFL governments, and one caretaker government over 14 years before the military take-over in 1962. Indonesia (independence in 1949): one parliamentary election and seven cabinets under a single head of state over 16 years before the mass violence that brought the military to power. Cambodia (independence in 1954): four elections, one governing party, and one head of state over 16 years before the 1970 military coup. Republic of Vietnam (independence in 1955): one head of state for 13 years followed by two military coups and a single election in 20 years before total collapse. The partial exception is the Philippines (independence in 1946): regular elections and alternating governing parties for 26 years until martial law was declared in 1972.

Less clear, however, is how the development and adherence to democratic institutions, norms, and participation were achieved and the prospects for their maintenance. For some authors, combinations of charismatic leadership, the internalization of liberal values, and even institutional design hold explanatory power. For other observers, profligate withdrawals from the petroleum fund, in violation of the sustainable income rule, and promises of future prosperity, based on a questionable strategy of state-led economic growth, hold the key. And with finite petroleum reserves, the sustainability of that strategy looms like a dark cloud. Scaling back or even abandoning capital-intensive projects such as the Petroleum Corridor and ZEESM may result in a twinge of regret and some local disappointment, but will have no grave political implications. By contrast, reducing the guaranteed outlays for lifetime pensions and expensive subsidies will come at a far greater political cost, and may prove impossible.

Timor-Leste's democratic success has been built on a ruling strategy of purchase, but without a corresponding effort to create a consolidated political machine. That few Timorese have been immune to the short-term temptations of cash transfers, subsidies, and, for the lucky few, contracts does not mean that the majority are persuaded by the merits and long-term prospects of that strategy. When a genuine movement to leadership by a younger generation does occur, short-term acquiescence based on material inducements will surely be tested by the necessary constraints of more prudent fiscal policy and the threat posed by those who have, or claim to have, expertise in the use of violence.

7 Future Research Agendas

The account of political dynamics in Timor-Leste developed in the preceding sections has been constructed around the dominant mode of relations between states and society, rulers and ruled, over four distinct periods. While highlighting the weight and residues of history, this account has inevitably privileged contrasts: *coercion* under colonial and neocolonial rule; *consent* expressed through the 1999 referendum and assumed under UN tutelage; *constraints* operating during the Fretilin government from 2002 until the crisis; and *purchase* under the Gusmão-led governments from 2007 until the present. Of these, inducements based on direct cash transfers, subsidies, and other forms of government largesse may be the easiest to deliver but, in conditions of finite resources, the most difficult to sustain.

Before considering future research agendas, it is necessary to note two peculiar features of the study of politics in Timor-Leste. First, if we exclude the literature on the United Nations missions, which is mostly the work of individuals with little or no country expertise, political scientists have been underrepresented in the enormous outpouring of scholarship produced on Timor-Leste since 1999. Anthropologists and individuals from "area studies" (as opposed to disciplinary) backgrounds have been most prominent, perhaps followed by those trained in development studies. Second, and reflecting a broader pattern in Southeast Asia in general and Indonesia in particular (Sidel 2015), a great deal of knowledge production (including some of the very best) on Timor-Leste has been done by practitioners who worked for the UN missions or by (and for) nonacademic institutions such as the World Bank, election-watch organizations, aid agencies, the International Crisis Group and nongovernmental organizations. These two features have exerted contradictory pushes and pulls on the study of politics. On the one hand, political scientists have held (too) tightly to the state-/nation-building and transitional justice lenses; on the other, they have devoted excessive attention to coverage of national events – the 2006 crisis, elections – and annual updates at the expense of processes of sociological change.

While state-building has provided the dominant approach to the study of Timor-Leste, with the exception of the security sector, surprisingly little attention has been paid to specific institutions and their internal dynamics. Absent is any serious consideration of the recruitment, socialization, and political proclivities of the civil service and other public sector employees. As noted earlier, despite an initial commitment to a lean administration, there has been a dramatic expansion in the number of government employees (public administration, health, education, etc.) from 17,412 in 2004 to 42,051 in 2010, and further expanding to 52,647 in 2017.[23] While government officials have justified this in terms of increasing state capacity, recruitment raises concerns about expanding patron–client relations and nepotism, and beyond that the emergence of a bureaucratic caste. Scholars may also wish to pay greater attention to the Secretariat of State for State Administration and its efforts to create a corporate identity. A related area in need of research is the 2014 law on Administrative Deconcentration that transformed the district administrative units into municipalities and granted their heads larger budgets. At stake are both the quality of service delivery, recruitment and staffing, and impacts that municipal budgetary discretion may have on political allegiances and voting behavior. A third area concerns the capacity and dynamics of the ministries and other state agencies. The few existing studies have been conducted by or under the auspices of international development agencies, and particularly the World

---

[23] The number of employees in state-owned enterprises (the state television company, electrical company, etc.) rose from 1,731 in 2010 to 13,144 in 2015.

Bank (Barma et al. 2014, part IV), and are often by authors who have worked as international advisors to the ministries about which they write. These works provide a wealth of detail available only to individuals embedded inside ministries and with intimate knowledge of East Timorese officials, but are often restricted in scope and may understate how the dynamics they identify relate to broader trajectories and strategies of rule.

Since the restoration of independence, the nongovernmental organization Timor-Leste Institute for Development Monitoring and Analysis/La'o Hamutuk has provided a tremendous public service by tracking and posting on its website detailed information on the state budget, including withdrawals from the Petroleum Fund and proposed, passed, and rectified budgets. Drawing on this wealth of data, La'o Hamutuk's Charles Scheiner has modelled Timor-Leste's state expenditures against the Petroleum Fund and the estimated future oil and gas production. In a 2015 article based on current spending and a set of "rosy assumptions," he estimated that "by 2026, before today's infants finish secondary school, the [Petroleum] Fund will be used up, and state spending will have to be slashed by more than two-thirds from desired levels" (Scheiner 2015: 92). From these resources and the government's transparency portal, there is much scope for researchers to examine state expenditures and the granting of state contracts, along with the policy framework and political interests that inform them.

Of pressing importance for Timor-Leste, and with latent political ramifications, is a broad range of demographic issues that have only been noted in passing in the above analysis. Birth, infant mortality, and total population growth rates all remain high, despite a decade of progress. With the population increasing by nearly 50 percent since the restoration of independence,[24] the population is extremely young and youth unemployment inordinately high. Alongside this, the percentage of the labor force engaged in agriculture has fallen and urbanization has accelerated rapidly. The population of the capital is now estimated at a quarter of a million people, or 20 percent of the national total, and is roughly ten times that of the next largest urban center, Baucau. A decade ago one prominent politician predicted that economic growth under AMP would be so rapid that the country would need to bring in migrant workers. He was wrong about the cause, but there has indeed been an influx of construction workers from China to work on PRC-funded projects and others seeking business opportunities. Elsewhere, the problem is agricultural stagnation and an exodus of young people to the United Kingdom, Ireland, and Indonesia in

---

[24] In July 2002 the government estimated the population to be 952,000, but the 2004 census found 923,000; in 2018 the figure is estimated to be 1.32 million.

search of opportunities (McWilliam 2015). So great are these changes in rural settlements and urban density that they will inevitably impact not only conceptions of "house" membership and attachments to place, but also notions of belonging in the national project. How these demographic and sociological processes relate to political aspirations and participation is worthy of further study.

On the other side of the sociological coin, political scientists would benefit from serious study of elite formation and transformation. The absence of such analysis is particularly surprising given the centrality that the generation of 1975 has had in explaining conflict and that Gusmão's revolutionary "charisma" has enjoyed in some studies as a source of national stability, if not unity. Since the restoration of independence, the salience of traditional rulers has quickly faded in the face of the veterans' bloc. Monarchism, which found momentary expression in 2002–2006, has lost traction against the rise of more universal appeals to traditional dress, ceremonial practice, and the deployment of elders. But neither is wholly spent. Insofar as class is reproduced through the family, greater attention might be paid to marriage patterns among the Dili elite (in which foreign spouses – overwhelmingly wives – have been particularly prominent) and links to regional networks of dynastic rulers, veterans, and other local notables. Of equal importance is how elites, including veterans with little formal education or experience managing money, socialize their children and the expectations that members of this next generation develop about their place in a very small and stratified society. Finally, in light of the significant pensions and contracts, what do patterns of consumption and investment (including overseas investment) reveal about elites and their faith in current government policy and Timor-Leste's future?

Lastly, there has been a glaring scholarly neglect of East Timorese political thinking. In part this may be a function of the multiplicity of sources – "tradition," "revolutionary" ideas both borrowed and developed in the 1970s, Lusophone constitutionalism, universal human rights, neoliberal economic orthodoxy, development discourse, and the mélange of political science East Timorese students have been exposed to while studying overseas, to name a few of the most obvious. In part, too, it reflects the power of stereotypes: Gusmão is seen as the bearer of charisma before he is considered an original thinker; Alkatiri is reduced to a technocratic socialist; and young intellectuals are treated as recipients of "foreign" knowledge rather than producers of ideas in their own right. A number of topics present themselves for consideration. What ideas do East Timorese – including both individual figures and larger collectivities –

have about the relationship between the state and markets? What does "decon-centration" mean in light of the distinction between administrative and political structures? What does the promotion of female representation in politics, which has been remarkably successful in Timor-Leste, mean to voters, and how are women who hold office treated? How does constitutionalism intersect with popular understandings of political legitimacy?

Glossary

AMP *Aliança de Maioria Parlamentar* (Parliamentary Majority Alliance)

Apodeti *Associação Popular Democrática Timorense* (Popular Democratic Association of Timorese)

ASDT *Associação Social Democratica Timor* (Social Democratic Association of Timor, established in 1974; reformed in 1999)

CAVR *Comissão de Acolhimento, Verdade e Reconciliação* (Commission on Reception, Truth and Reconciliation)

CNRT *Conselho Nacional de Resistência Timorense* (National Council for Timorese Resistance, est. 1998)

CNRT *Congresso Nacional de Reconstrução de Timor* (National Congress of Timorese Reconstruction, formed in 2007)

CPD-RDTL *Conselho Popular pela Defesa da República Democrática de Timor-Leste* (Popular Council for the Defense of the Democratic Republic of Timor-Leste)

Falintil *Forças Armadas de Libertação Nacional de Timor-Leste* (Armed Forces for the National Liberation of East Timor)

FDTL *Força de Defesa de Timor-Leste* (East Timor Defense Force); later changed to *Falintil-Força de Defesa de Timor-Leste* (F-FDTL)

firaku collective term for people from the eastern districts

Fretilin *Frente Revolucionária de Timor Leste Independente* (Revolutionary Front of Independent East Timor)

kaladi collective term for people from the western districts

KHUNTO *Kmanek Haburas Unidade Nacional Timor Oan* (Enrich the National Unity of the Sons of Timor)

PD *Partido Democrático* (Democratic Party)

PLP *Partido Libertação Popular* (People's Liberation Party)

PNTL *Polícia Nacional de Timor-Leste* (East Timor National Police)

PSD *Partido Social Democrata* (Social Democratic Party)

UDT   *União Democrática Timorense* (Timorese Democratic Union)

ZEESM   *Zonas Especiais de Economia Social de Mercado* (Special Zones of the Social Market Economy of Timor-Leste)

Bibliography

Newspapers and Magazines

Australian Broadcasting Corporation (ABC)
Independente
Suara Timor Lorosae (STL)
Sydney Morning Herald (SMH)
Talitakum
Timor Post
UNOTIL Daily Media Review
Vox Populi

Documents

Australian Federal Police (2008). Intelligence Advisory Report: Operation Oportet: Forensic ballistics examination results, document 5547919, dated November 27, 2008.

National Council of Timorese Resistance (CNRT) (1998). Magna Carta concerning Freedoms, Rights, Duties and Guarantees for the People of East Timor. English version available at www.easttimorlawandjusticebulletin .com/2009/01/east-timors-magna-carta.html (accessed March 5, 2018).

(1999). Managing the Transitional Administration in East Timor, with cover letter signed by Xanana Gusmão, October 19, 1999.

Independent Evaluation Group (2011). Timor-Leste Country Program Evaluation, 2000–2010, Washington DC: Independent Evaluation Group, The World Bank. Available at https://openknowledge.worldbank.org/bit stream/handle/10986/22736/Timor0Leste0000valuation00200002010.pdf? sequence=1&isAllowed=y.

Taur Matan Ruak (2016). Speech by his excellency the President of the Republic, Taur Matan Ruak, to national parliament, on the dismissal of Major-General Lere Anan Timur, February 25, posted at https://aitaraklar anlive.wordpress.com/2016/02/26/speech-by-his-excellency-the-presi dent-of-the-republic-taur-matan-ruak-to-national-parliament-on-the-dis missal-of-major-general-lere-anan-timur/ (accessed May 25, 2018).

United Nations (1999). Agreement between the Republic of Indonesia and the Portuguese Republic on the Question of East Timor, 5 May 1999, Annex I in United Nations, Question of East Timor: Report of the Secretary General,

May 5, 1999, available at https://peaceaccords.nd.edu/sites/default/files/accords/East_Timor_Peace_Agreement-1999.pdf (accessed March 5, 2018).

United Nations Security Council (1999). Resolution No. 1272, October 25, available at http://dag.un.org/handle/11176/36759 (accessed March 5, 2018).

Democratic Republic of Timor-Leste Publications

Direcção Nacional de Estatística (2006). *Censo da população e habitação 2004*, Dili: Gráfica Pátria.

República Democrática de Timor-Leste (2002). *Constitution of the Democratic Republic of East Timor*, available in English at http://timor-leste.gov.tl/wp-content/uploads/2010/03/Constitution_RDTL_ENG.pdf

República Democrática de Timor-Leste, Planning Commission (2002). East Timor: State of the Nation Report. Dili.

República Democrática de Timor-Leste, Governo (2003a). *Timor-Leste: Ita iha nebe ona ohin loron*, Dili: Grafica, Patria.

República Democrática de Timor-Leste, Planning and External Assistance Management Division, Ministry of Planning and Finance (2003b). *Timor-Leste: Poverty in a new nation: Analysis for action.*

República Democrática de Timor-Leste, Ministério da Administração Estatal (2003c). Local Government Options Study Draft Report.

República Democrática de Timor-Leste (2005). Prime Minister, media release "Timor-Leste established Petroleum Fund," September 23, 2005, posted at www.laohamutuk.org/OilWeb/Finances/PetFund/PFEstablished.htm.

República Democrática de Timor-Leste (2008). "Integração dos ex-militares na vida civil," Decree 12/2008, dated 11 June 2008; posted at www.mj.gov.tl/jornal/?q=node/1016 (accessed May 26, 2018).

República Democrática de Timor-Leste, Ministério das Finanças (2014). Briefing note to respond to "The resource curse in Timor-Leste" article authored by Charles Scheiner (La'o Hamutuk), National Directorate of Economic Policy, September 2.

Journal Articles and Books

Allard, T. (2016). "Discontent" about Xanana Gusmao, Mari Alkatiri families: East Timor President, Sydney Morning Herald, February 27, posted at www.smh.com.au/world/discontent-about-xanana-gusmao-mari-alkatiri-families-east-timor-president-20160226-gn4ck9.html (accessed May 25, 2018).

Amnesty International (2003). The Democratic Republic of Timor Leste: A new police service – a new beginning, London: Amnesty International.

Anderson, T. (2003). Self-determination after independence: East Timor and the World Bank, *Portuguese Studies Review* 11(1): 169–185.

(2010). Cuban health cooperation in Timor-Leste and the South West Pacific, in *South-south cooperation: A challenge to the aid system*, Quezon City: IBON Books, 77–86.

Arnold, M. (2010). Timor-Leste: The window for a "normal" future?, *Asian Survey* 51(1): 215–220.

Asia Foundation (2014). Timor-Leste public opinion poll. Posted at http://asiafoun dation.org/resources/pdfs/PublicOpinionPollResultsMarch2014ENGLISH .pdf.

Aspinall, E., Hicken A., Scambary J., and Weiss, M. (2018). Timor-Leste votes: parties and patronage, *Journal of Democracy* 29(1): 153–167.

Babo-Soares, D. (2003). Branching from the Trunk: East Timorese Perceptions of Nationalism in Transition, Ph.D. Dissertation, Australian National University.

(2004). *Nahe Biti*: the philosophy and process of grassroots reconciliation (and justice) in East Timor, *Asia Pacific Journal of Anthropology* 5(1): 15–33.

Ball, D. (2002). Defence of East Timor: A recipe for disaster? *Global Change, Peace & Security* 14(3): 175–189.

Barma, N., Huybens E., and Viñuela, L. (2014). Institutions taking root: Building state capacity in challenging contexts, Washington, DC: World Bank.

Beauvais, J. (2001). Benevolent despotism: A critique of U.N. state-building in East Timor, *New York University Journal of International Law and Politics* 33(4): 1101–1178.

Beuman, L. (2016). *Political institutions in East Timor: Semi-presidentialism and democratisation*, London and New York: Routledge.

Blunt, P. (2009). The political-economy of accountability in Timor-Leste: Implications for public policy, *Public Administration and Development*, 29(2): 89–100.

Boughton, B. (2008). Unraveling the East Timor Assassination Story: Republic's rebel with friends in high places, *The Australian*, 16 February.

Bovensiepen, J. (2015). *The land of gold: Post-conflict recovery and cultural revival in independent Timor-Leste*, Ithaca, NY: Cornell Southeast Asia Program.

Bovensiepen, J., ed. (2018). *The promise of progress: visions of the future in Timor-Leste*, Canberra: ANU Press.

Centre for Defence Studies (2000). Independent study on security force options for East Timor, London: The Centre for Defence Studies, King's College.

Chesterman, S. (2004). Building democracy through benevolent autocracy. In E. Newman and R. Rich, eds., *The UN Role in Promoting Democracy: Between Ideals and Reality*, Tokyo: United Nations University Press, pp. 86–112.

Chomsky, N. (2006). Foreword, in R. Tanter, D. Ball, and G. van Klinken, *Masters of Terror: Indonesia's military and violence in East Timor*, Lanham, MD: Rowman and Littlefield, pp. ix–xiii.

Chopra, J. (2002). Building state failure in East Timor, *Development and Change* 33(5): 979–1000.

Cohen, D. (2003). *Intended to fail: The trials before the Ad Hoc Human Rights Court in Jakarta*, New York: International Center for Transitional Justice.

Comissão de Acolhimento Verdade e Reconciliação de Timor-Leste (CAVR) (2013). *Chega! The Report of the Commission for Reception, Truth and Reconciliation*, Dili: CAVR.

Cotton, J. (2007). Timor-Leste and the discourse of state failure, *Australian Journal of International Affairs* 61(4): 455–470.

Devereux, A. (2015). *Timor-Leste's bill of rights: A preliminary history.* Canberra: ANU Press.

Drysdale, J. (2007). Sustainable development or resource cursed? An exploration of Timor-Leste's institutional choices, PhD. thesis, The Australian National University.

East Timor Law and Justice Bulletin (2010). Timor police say a new coup plot from CPD-RDTL and Bua Malus, March 3, posted at www.easttimorla wandjusticebulletin.com/2010/03/timor-police-say-new-coup-plot-from-cpd.html (accessed May 27, 2018).

Economist Intelligence Unit (EIU) (2018). Democracy Index 2017: Free speech under attack, posted at www.eiu.com.libproxy1.nus.edu.sg/Handlers/ WhitepaperHandler.ashx?fi=Democracy_Index_2017.pdf&mode= wp&campaignid=DemocracyIndex2017 (accessed May 22, 2018).

Engel, R. (2015). The state, society and international interventions in Timor-Leste: creating conditions for violence, PhD. thesis, SOAS.

Feijó, R. (2013). Timor-Leste in 2013: Marching on its own feet, *Asian Survey* 54(1): 83–88.

(2016). *Dynamics of democracy in Timor-Leste: The birth of a democratic nation, 1999–2012*, Amsterdam: University of Amsterdam Press.

(2018). Timor-Leste in 2017: Between a diplomatic victory and the return of "belligerent democracy," *Asian Survey* 58(1): 206–212.

Fitzpatrick, D. (2000). Re-establishing land titles and administration in East Timor, *Pacific Economic Bulletin* 15(2): 152–160.

Fitzpatrick, D., McWilliam A., and Barnes S. (2012). *Property and social resilience in times of conflict: Land, custom and law in East Timor*, London and New York: Routledge.

Goldstone, A. (2004). UNTAET with Hindsight: The peculiarities of politics in an incomplete state, *Global Governance* 10: 83–98.

(2013). Building a state and "state-building": East Timor and the UN, 1999–2012. In M. Berdal and D. Zaum, eds., *Political economy of state-building: power after peace*, London and New York: Routledge.

Gorjão, P. (2002). The legacy and lessons of the United Nations Transitional Administration in East Timor, *Contemporary Southeast Asia* 24(2): 313–336.

Gorjão, P., and Monteiro, A. (2009). Is Timor-Leste a failed state? *Portuguese Journal of International Affairs* 1: 12–21.

Grenfell, L. (2009). Promoting the rule of law in Timor-Leste, *Conflict, Security and Development* 9(2): 213–238.

Gunn, G. C. (2007). The state of East Timor studies after 1999, *Journal of Contemporary Asia* 37(1): 95–114.

(2010). Timor-Leste in 2009: Cup half full or half empty? *Asian Survey* 50(1): 235–240.

Gusmão, X. (1982). Message to the 37th United Nations General Assembly. In S. Niner, ed. 2000, pp. 74–84.

(1986). A history that beats in the Maubere Soul. In S. Niner, ed. 2000, pp. 85–126.

(1998). New Year Message for 1999. In S. Niner, ed. 2000, pp. 224–235.

(2003). Address by H. E. President Kay Rala Xanana Gusmão, Xanana on the occasion of the International Conference on Traditional Conflict Resolution and Traditional Justice in Timor-Leste, Dili, June 27.

(2005). *Timor Lives! Speeches of freedom and independence*, Alexandria, New South Wales: Longueville Media.

Guterres, J. C. (2008). Timor-Leste: A year of democratic elections, *Southeast Asian Affairs*: 359–372.

Hill, H., and Saldanha, J. (2001). *East Timor: Development Challenges for the World's Newest Nation*, Singapore: ISEAS.

Hohe, T. (2002). The clash of paradigms: International administration and local political legitimacy in East Timor, *Contemporary Southeast Asia* 24(3): 569–589.

Hohe, T., and Nixon, R. (2003). *Reconciling justice: "Traditional" law and state judiciary in Timor-Leste*, Dili: United States Institute of Peace.

Hughes, C. (2009). *Dependent Communities: Aid and Politics in Cambodia and East Timor*, Ithaca, NY: Cornell Southeast Asia Program.

Hunt, Janet (2004). Building a new society: NGOs in East Timor. *New Community Quarterly* 2(1): 16–23.

Hyland, T., and L. Murdoch (2002). East Timor celebrates as a nation is born, *The Age*, May 20.

Ingram, S., L. Kent, and A. McWilliam (2015). *A new era? Timor-Leste after the UN*, Canberra: ANU Press.

Independente (2018). "Timor-Leste's veterans stand by Alkatiri," October 25, posted at www.independente.tl/tl/nasional/timor-leste-s-veterans-stand-by-alkatiri-government (accessed January 13, 2018).

International Crisis Group (2006). Resolving Timor-Leste's crisis, Dili/Brussels: Asia Report No. 120.

(2007). Timor-Leste's parliamentary elections, Dili/Brussels: Update briefing No. 65.

(2009). Timor-Leste: No time for complacency, Dili/Brussels: Asia Briefing No. 97.

(2011). Timor-Leste's veterans: An unfinished struggle, Dili/Brussels: Asia Briefing No. 129.

Kammen, D. (2009). A tape-recorder and a wink? Transcript of the May 29, 1983 Meeting Between Governor Carrascalão and Xanana Gusmão, *Indonesia* 87: 73–102.

(2010). Subordinating Timor: Central authority and the origin of communal identities in East Timor, *Bijdragen tot de Tal-, Land- en Volkenkunde* 166 (2/3): 244–269.

(2011a). The armed forces in Timor-Leste: Politicization through elite conflict, in M. Mietzner, ed., *The political resurgence of the military in Southeast Asia: Conflict and leadership*, London and NY: Routledge, pp. 107–125.

(2011b). Sovereignty and food politics in East Timor, *Kasarinlan: Philippine Journal of Third World Studies* 26 (1–2): 264–273.

(2012). Between violence and negotiation: Rethinking the Indonesian occupation and East Timorese resistance, in M. Miller, ed., *Autonomy and Armed Separatism in South and Southeast Asia*, Singapore: Institute of Southeast Asian Studies, pp. 93–112.

Kammen, D., and Hayati, S. (2007). Crisis and Rice in East Timor, *CounterPunch*, March 5.

Katzenstein, S. (2003). Hybrid tribunals: Searching for justice in East Timor, *Harvard Human Rights Journal* 16: 245–278.

Kent, L. (2012). *The dynamics of transitional justice: International models and local realities in East Timor*, Oxon and New York: Routledge.

Kent, L., and Kinsella, N. (2015). The veterans' valorisation scheme: Marginalising women's contributions to the resistance. In S. Ingram et al. 2015, pp. 213–223.

Kent, L., and Wallis, J. (2014). Timor-Leste's veterans' pension scheme: Who are the beneficiaries and who is missing out? The State, Society and Governance Programme in Melanesia, In Brief 2014/13, https://openresearch-repository.anu.edu.au/bitstream/1885/143160/1/SSGM_IB_2014_13_KentWallis_Print&Web.pdf (accessed May 26, 2018).

King, D. (2003). East Timor's founding elections and emerging party system, *Asian Survey* 43(5): 745–757.

Kingsbury, D. (2009). *East Timor: The price of freedom*, New York: Palgrave-Macmillan.

(2010). National identity in Timor-Leste: Challenges and opportunities, *South East Asia Research* 18(1): 133–159.

(2017). Is East Timor run by a "stable" govt or conspiratorial oligarchy, dated January 27, 2017, posted at https://blogs.deakin.edu.au/deakin-speaking/2017/01/27/is-east-timor-run-by-a-stable-govt-or-conspiratorial-oligarchy/ (accessed February 11, 2017).

La'o Hamutuk (2002). Excerpts from East Timor's combined sources budget 2002–2003, presented at May 2002 donor's conference, posted at www.laohamutuk.org/OilWeb/Finances/budget%202002–3.htm (accessed May 28, 2018).

(2009). How much money have international donors spent on and in Timor-Leste, posted at www.laohamutuk.org/reports/09bgnd/HowMuchAidEn.pdf (accessed April 16, 2018).

(2013). The national impact of benefits for former combatants, posted at www.laohamutuk.org/econ/pension/VetPension6Mar2013en.pps (accessed May 26, 2018).

Leach, M. (2009). The 2007 presidential and parliamentary elections in Timor-Leste, *Australian Journal of Politics and History*, 55(2): 219–232.

(2013). Timor-Leste in 2012 beyond international statebuilding? *Asian Survey* 53(1): 156–161.

(2014). Concerns over judicial independence in Timor-Leste, *EastAsiaForum*, October 31. Posted at www.eastasiaforum.org/2014/10/31/concerns-over-judicial-independence-in-timor-leste/ (accessed May 28, 2018).

Martin, I., and Mayer-Reickh, A. (2005). The United Nations and East Timor: From self-determination to state-building, *International Peacekeeping* 12(1): 125–145.

McWilliam, A. (2005). Houses of resistance in East Timor: Structuring sociality in the new nation, *Anthropological Forum* 15(1): 27–44.

(2007). Introduction: Restorative custom: Ethnographic perspectives on conflict and local justice in Timor, *The Asia Pacific Journal of Anthropology* 8(1): 1–8.

(2015). Rural-urban inequalities and migration in Timor-Leste. In S. Ingram et al. 2015, pp. 225–234.

Meitzner Yoder, L. (2015). The development eraser: Fantastical schemes, aspirational distractions and high modern mega-events in the Oecusse enclave, Timor-Leste, *Journal of Political Ecology* 22: 299–321.

Mendes, P. (2008). Timor-Leste: The unsustainable island, *Publico*, 25 November, posted at http://jornal.publico.clix.pt/main.asp?dt=20081125&id.

Moxham, B. (2008). State-making and the post-conflict city: Integration in Dili, disintegration in Timor-Leste, London: Crisis States Working Papers, no. 2, Development Studies Institute, London School of Economics.

Mubyarto, S., Hudiyanto, L., Djatmiko, E., Setiawati, I., and Mawarni, A. (1991). *East Timor: The Impact of Integration*, Australia: Gadjah Mada University Research Centre for Village and Regional Development and Indonesian Resources and Information Program.

Murdoch, L. (2008) "Timor collides with its future," *The Sydney Morning Herald*, November 22.

Neves, G. (2011). Timor: Where Has All the Aid Gone?, *Foreign Policy in Focus*, June 20, posted at http://fpif.org/timor_where_has_all_the_aid_gone/ (accessed April 30, 2018).

(2013). Timor-Leste: The political economy of a rentier state, presented at Timor-Leste Studies Association, 2013, posted at www.laohamutuk.org/econ/model/NevesPoliticalRentierTLSA2013.pdf.

Niner, S. (2000). *To Resist is to Win: The autobiography of Xanana Gusmão*, Richmond, Victoria: Aurora Books.

Nolan, C. (2015). After Xanana: Challenges for stability. In S. Ingram et al. 2015, pp. 155–168.

Nygaard-Christensen, M. (2016). Timor-Leste in 2015: Petro-politics or sustainable growth, *Southeast Asian Affairs 2016*, Singapore: ISEAS, pp. 347–359.

Pereira, A. (2009). The Dreams of Kay Rala Xanana Gusmão, posted at www .etan.org/et2009/02february/22/19dreams.htm (accessed May 25, 2018).

Pushkina, D., and Maier, P. (2012). United Nations Peace-keeping in Timor-Leste, *Civil Wars* 14(3): 324–343.

Rees, E. (2002). Security sector reform and transitional administrations, *Conflict, Security and Development* 2(1): 151–156.

(2004). Under pressure: Falintil – Forças de Defesa de Timor Leste: Three decades of defence force development in Timor Leste, 1975–2004, Geneva: Working Paper No. 139, Geneva Centre for the Democratic Control of Armed Forces.

Robinson, G. (2010). *"If you leave us here we will die": How genocide was stopped in East Timor*, Princeton: Princeton University Press.

(2011). East Timor ten years on: Legacies of violence, *Journal of Asian Studies* 70(4): 1007–1021.

Rohland, K., and Cliffe, S. (2002). The East Timor reconstruction program: Successes, problems and tradeoffs, World Bank Conflict Prevention and Reconstruction Unit Working Paper Series no. 2, November.

Roosa, J. (2007). How does a truth commission find out what the truth is? The case of East Timor's CAVR, *Pacific Affairs* 80(4): 569–80.

Sahe Institute for Liberation (2003). "Memerdekakan rakyat setelah memperoleh tanah air," *Libertasan* 2.

Scambary, J. (2007). Disaffected groups and social movements in East Timor, unpublished research paper for AusAID.

(2009). Anatomy of a conflict: the 2006–2007 communal violence in East Timor, *Conflict, Security & Development*, 9(2): 265–288.

(2015). In search of white elephants: The political economy of resource income expenditure in East Timor, *Critical Asian Studies*, 47(2): 283–308.

Scheiner, C. (2015). Can the petroleum fund exorcise the resource curse from Timor-Leste. In S. Ingram et al. 2015, pp. 73–101.

Schofield, C. (2007). Minding the gap: The Australia-East Timor treaty on certain maritime arrangements in the Timor Sea (CMATS), *The International Journal of Marine and Coastal Law* 22(2); 189–234.

Shoesmith, D. (2003). Timor-Leste: Divided leadership in a semi-presidential system, *Asian Survey*, 43(2): 231–252.

(2011). Timor-Leste: On the path to peace and prosperity? In *Southeast Asian Affairs 2011*, Singapore: ISEAS, pp. 332–335.

(2017). Timor-Leste in 2016: Redefining democracy. In *Southeast Asian Affairs 2017*, Singapore: ISEAS, pp. 387–404.

Sidel, J. (2015). Sojourn symposium review essay, *Sojourn* 30(1): 256–261.

Simonsen, S. (2006). The authoritarian temptation in East Timor: Nationbuilding and the need for inclusive governance, *Asian Survey*, 46(4): 575–596.

Smith, A. (2004). Timor-Leste: Strong government, weak state. In *Southeast Asian Affairs 2004*, Singapore: ISEAS, pp. 279–294.

Soares, A. (2015). A social movement as an antidote to corruption. In S. Ingram et al. 2015, pp. 203–212.

(2004). Peranan gerakan bawah tanah dalam proses perjuangan pembebasan nasional Timor-Leste (studi kasus di sub-region Viqueque wilayah Baucau dan Viqueque dari tahun 1979–1994), BA thesis, Universitas Nasional Timor-Leste.

Sousa, I. (2001). The Portuguese colonization and the problem of East Timorese nationalism, *Lusotropie* 2001: 183–194.

Suhrke, A. (2001). Peacekeepers as nation-builders: Dilemmas of the UN in East Timor, *International Peacekeeping* 8(4): 1–20.

Timor-Leste Armed Violence Assessment 1 (2008), Dealing with the Kilat.

Traube, E. (2007). Unpaid wages: Local narratives and the imagination of the nation, *The Asia Pacific Journal of Anthropology* 8(1): 9–25.

United Nations High Commissioner for Human Rights (2006). Report of the United Nations Independent Special Commission of Inquiry for Timor-Leste, Geneva: UNHCHR.

Van der Auweraert, P. (2012). Dealing with the 2006 internal displacement crisis in Timor-Leste: Between reparations and humanitarian policymaking, International Center for Transitional Justice and Brookings-LSE Project on Internal Displacement, posted at www.ictj.org/sites/default/files/ICTJ-Brookings-Displacement-Timor-Leste-CaseStudy-2012-English.pdf.

Wallis, J. (2012). A liberal-local hybrid peace project in action? The increasing engagement between the local and the liberal in Timor-Leste, *Review of International Studies* 38(4): 735–761.

(2015). Assessing the implementation and impact of Timor-Leste's cash payment schemes. In S. Ingram et al. 2015, pp. 235–249.

Wigglesworth, A. (2017). Youth in search of a future: Urban drift, education and work in Timor-Leste, *Development Bulletin* 78, ANU Development Studies Network. Posted at http://ssgm.bellschool.anu. edu.au/sites/default/files/ publications/attachments/2017–09/development_bulletin_78_ web_version.pdf#page=103

Wilson, B. (2012). To 2012 and beyond: international assistance to police and security sector development, *Asia Politics and Policy* 4(1): 73–88.

History

The major Portuguese histories of Timor-Leste are A. Faria de Morias, *Subsídios para a História de Timor*, Goa: Tipografia Rangel-Bastorá, 1934; Luna de Oliveira, *Timor na Historia de Portugal*, Vol. 1–4, Lisbon: Agencia Geral das Colonias, 1949; and A. Matos, *Timor Português 1515–1769: Contribuição para a sua História*, Lisbon: Instituto Histórico Infante Dom Henrique, 1974. There are a several important challenges to the imperial historiography. For the sixteenth to eighteenth centuries, see H. Hägerdal, *Lords of the Land, Lords of the Sea: Conflict and adaption in early colonial Timor, 1600–1800*, Leiden: KITLV Press, 2012. For the period 1850 to 1912, see Katharine G. Davidson, "The Portuguese Colonisation of Timor: The Final Stage, 1850–1912," PhD. Dissertation, University of Western Australia, 1994, and R. Pélissier, *Timor en guerre: Le crocodile et les Portugais (1847–1913)*, Orgeval, France: 1996. The only comprehensive English-language histories are G. Gunn's encyclopedic *Timor Loro Sae: 500 Years*. Macau: 1999, and F. Durand, *History of Timor-Leste*, Chiang Mai: Silkworm Books, 2016.

The best accounts of the aborted decolonization in 1974–75 and the Indonesian invasion are J. Dunn, *East Timor: A rough passage to independence*, Australia: Longueville Media, 2003; J. Jolliffe, *East Timor: Nationalism and colonialism*, St. Lucia: University of Queensland, 1978; B. Nicol, *The stillborn nation*, Melbourne: Visa Books, 1978; and H. Hill, *Stirrings of Nationalism in East Timor: Fretilin 1974–1978: The Origins, Ideologies and Strategies of a Nationalist Movement*, Otford, New South Wales: Otford Press, 2002. The most complete Indonesian account of the period is Soekanto, ed., *Integrasi: Kebulatan tekad rakyat Timor Timur*, Jakarta: Yayasan Parikesit, 1976.

The major studies of the Indonesian occupation are C. Budiardjo and S. L. Liem, *The War Against East Timor*, London: Zed Books, 1984, and J. Taylor, *Indonesia's Forgotten War: The Hidden History of East Timor*, London: Zed Books, 1991, both with an emphasis on human rights abuses. By far the best work on the violence in 1999 is G. Robinson's *"If you leave us here we will die": How genocide was stopped in East Timor*, Princeton: Princeton University Press, 2009. See also Ian Martin, *Self-determination in East Timor: The United Nations, the ballot, and international intervention*, Boulder and London: Lynne Rienner Publishers, 2001, and R. Tanter, D. Ball, and G. van Klinken, *Masters of Terror: Indonesia's military and violence in East Timor*, Lanham, MD: Rowman and Littlefield, 2006. The most sophisticated account by an Indonesian military officer is K. Syahnakri's *Timor Timur: The untold story*, Jakarta: Kompas, 2013.

Biographies and Autobiographies

For an English translation of part of Xanana Gusmão's autobiography and other selected writings, see *To Resist Is to Win! The Autobiography of Xanana Gusmão*, S. Niner, ed., Richmond, Victoria: Aurora Books, 2000. For a biography of Gusmão up to 1999, S. Niner, *Xanana: Leader of the Struggle for Independent Timor-Leste*, Melbourne: Australian Scholarly Publishing, 2009.

On the life of Mario Viegas Carrascalão, who was a founding member of UDT in 1975 and served as governor of occupied East Timor from 1982 until 1992, see his heartfelt autobiography *Timor: Antes do Futuro*, Dili: Livraria Mau Huran, 2006.

For the winners of the 1996 Nobel Peace Prize, see José Ramos-Horta's autobiographical *Funu: The unfinished saga of East Timor*, Lawrenceville, NJ: Red Sea Press, 1987, and A. Kohen, *From the place of the dead: Bishop Belo and the struggle for East Timor*, New York: St. Martin's Press, 1999.

Films

Dalan ba Damai [Road to Peace] (2005), a powerful 144-minute documentary, produced by filmmaker Ian White for the Commission for Reception, Truth and Reconcilation, in Tetum with subtitles available in English, Portuguese, and Indonesian.

The Diplomat (2000), an 84-minute documentary about José Ramos-Horta's diplomatic efforts for a free East Timor. www.emeraldfilms.com.au/?portfolio=diplomat

Answered by Fire (2006), a two-part television film based on Australian Federal police officer David Savage's book *Dancing with the Devil* about policing the 1999 referendum.

Balibo (2009), a dramatic account of the deaths of five Australian-based journalists covering the Indonesian invasion of Portuguese Timor in 1975, based on the book of the same title by journalist Jill Jolliffe.

A Guerra da Beatriz [Beatriz' War] (2013), feature-length film produced in Timor-Leste.

Reference and Electronic Resources

Durand, F. (2006). *East Timor: A country at the crossroads of Asia and the Pacific: A geo-historical atlas*. Bangkok: Silkworm Books.

Gunn, G. (2011). *Historical dictionary of East Timor*. Lanham: Scarecrow Press.

The Commission for Reception, Truth and Reconciliation's final report and a variety of other documentation are available at www.cavr-timorleste.org/.

East Timor Action Network (ETAN) includes archival and current information on human rights and justice, political affairs, the United Nations missions and presence, economic development, the environment, and other issues. Available at www.etan.org/.

Clearing House for Archival Records on Timor (Chart) hosts valuable historical documents and photographs. Available at https://timorarchives.word press.com/.

La'o Hamutuk, a nongovernmental organization based in Dili, has an extensive archive on its website, including annual state budgets, government documents, and media reports. Available at www.laohamutuk.org/.

The Timor Leste Studies Association runs an active mailing list that includes periodic bibliographical listings of new scholarship on Timor-Leste. Available at http://mailman.anu.edu.au/ mailman/listinfo/easttimorstudies.

The Timor-Leste government website http://timor-leste.gov.tl/?lang=en (also available in Tetum and Portuguese) includes a variety of information on the country, government structures, current policies, and audiovisual presentations. For the ambitious Timor-Leste Special Zone for Social Market Economy (ZEESM), see www.zeesm.tl/en/zeesm-tl-front-page-english/. On the national oil company and the south coast Tasi Mane project, official information is available at www.timorgap .com/databases/website.nsf/vwAll/FAQs.

Cambridge Elements ≡

Politics and Society in Southeast Asia

Edward Aspinall
Australian National University

Edward Aspinall is a professor of politics at the Coral Bell School of Asia-Pacific Affairs, Australian National University. A specialist of Southeast Asia, especially Indonesia, much of his research has focused on democratisation, ethnic politics and civil society in Indonesia and, most recently, clientelism across Southeast Asia.

Meredith L. Weiss
University at Albany, SUNY

Meredith L. Weiss is Professor of Political Science at the University at Albany, SUNY. Her research addresses political mobilization and contention, the politics of identity and development, and electoral politics in Southeast Asia, with particular focus on Malaysia and Singapore.

About the Series

The Elements series Politics and Society in Southeast Asia includes both country-specific and thematic studies on one of the world's most dynamic regions. Each title, written by a leading scholar of that country or theme, combines a succinct, comprehensive, up-to-date overview of debates in the scholarly literature with original analysis and a clear argument.

Cambridge Elements ≡

Politics and Society in Southeast Asia